# CHESTERFIELD
# TROLLEYBUSES

When members of the Tramways Committee travelled to inspect the Rotherham trolleybus system on 9 November 1912 they were driven along the route to Maltby in one of the RET single-deckers shown here, plying the only rural trackless line then in existence in Britain. (*Local Studies Library*)

# CHESTERFIELD TROLLEYBUSES

Barry M. Marsden

*Dedicated to Philip Moffat Robinson, for his faith in the viability of the trolleybus.*

TEMPUS

Not all ratepayers were convinced of the viability of the railless proposals, and a poll was called for 27 January 1913 to give opponents the chance to record their views. In the event 905 electors supported the Railless Traction Bill, while 383 voted against it. The scheme was eventually killed off by the war.

First published 2002
Copyright © Barry M. Marsden, 2002

Tempus Publishing Limited
The Mill, Brimscombe Port,
Stroud, Gloucestershire, GL5 2QG
www.tempus-publishing.com

ISBN 0 7524 2760 1

TYPESETTING AND ORIGINATION BY
Tempus Publishing Limited
PRINTED IN GREAT BRITAIN BY
Midway Colour Print, Wiltshire

# Contents

# Acknowledgements

Many individuals and institutions have provided assistance in the production of this work. Particular gratitude goes to Peter Stevenson at the Town Hall, who granted unlimited access to the borough archives, and to whom I owe a great debt for his interest and help. I must also thank the staff of the Tramway Museum Society at Crich, and Stuart Hislop, former manager of the now defunct Chesterfield Transport, who kindly allowed me to study the collection surviving from the old Corporation records. The staff of the Chesterfield Local Studies Library furnished support in my search through local newspapers and other source material. Other assistance has come from Roger Kaye, and other correspondents who have furnished photographs and other information used in the compilation of this book.

Would readers please note that references to the *Times* in this book relate to the *Derbyshire Times*.

# Introduction

I was born on St Valentine's Day 1938, a mere hundred yards from the nearest wires of the Corporation trolleybus system, and must have rode on more than one of the vehicles during the last few weeks of their working lives, though understandably I have no recollection of these occasions. At a tender age my parents moved to Hardwick Street, directly opposite the entrance to the transport department, though by that time the trackless fleet had been replaced by noisy, smelly motorbuses. I was a student at Sheffield in October 1960, and well remember a ride from Pond Street to the University during that last week of English tramcar operation. Strangely enough I was lecturing in Bradford a decade later when the city dispensed with its trolleybuses – the last to run in Britain.

This background must have awakened my interest in the history of electric traction in my native town, and the era of the trackless, or railless as Chesterfield Corporation invariably called them, is a short but fascinating period in the transport record of the borough. After the First World War the town's tramway undertaking was in serious trouble, with a fleet of decrepit tramcars, plus a worn-out track and overhead. By 1924 the Corporation were seeking to replace the ageing line with an alternative mode of transport, the options being either the trolleybus or the petrol omnibus. Two expert reports written for the council suggested that the former would be the preferred option for the town, as they would be cheaper to operate and could utilize the existing tramway poles. They could also run on locally generated electrical current produced from the fuel supplied by the region's coalfields.

However, the proposal set off a fierce battle with trackless opponents among the population, spurred on by the local press and dissenting council members spearheaded by Sir Ernest Shentall, former Chairman of the Tramways Committee. The latter body, led by Philip Moffat Robinson, forced through the trolleybus option in the teeth of much local animosity, yet though the vehicles were an undisputed success, they only enjoyed a ten year reign before being superseded by the cheaper diesel motorbus. This account of that momentous period has been very much a labour of love, and my hope is that the chronicle of this minor but significant enterprise will prove as absorbing to read as it was for me to research and write.

Barry M. Marsden
Eldwick, August 2002

On 11 December 1924 Philip Robinson, Tramways Committee Chairman, arranged a short demonstration by an AEC 602 trolleybus similar to the one in the photograph, and then on its way to Mexborough. The vehicle performed with its positive boom on the tram overhead, and a trailing skate in the track groove. (*Chesterfield Transport*)

# One
# Railless
# Recommendations
# 1912-1914

In November 1912 the Chesterfield Borough Council took the first steps towards increasing communication facilities between the township and the surrounding districts. The single linear tram route opened in December 1904 was the only one to be constructed despite hopes for extensions to Hasland and Birdholme. The latter expansions were now non-starters due to the heavy outlay in laying and maintaining the original cars and track, and cheaper alternatives were now sought. The augmentation of the system was a matter of civic pride and commercial calculation. The petrol bus was still clumsy and unreliable, but the advent of the trolleybus (the 'railless' or 'trackless' tram) under development on the Continent for a decade or so, offered another option as a mode of transport, one which might well be suitable for connecting the township with outlying villages. A hybrid mode of transport, the trolleybus needed no rails to run on, and was more flexible, having a limited manoeuvring capability. The catalyst for considering traffic extensions may well have been the inauguration by nearby Rotherham of a trackless route from the town centre to Maltby, a colliery village some eight miles away. After Robert Acland, the Tramways Manager, and Vincent Smith, the Borough Surveyor, had prepared a joint report on the subject, a full council meeting on 8 November resolved that 'it is expedient that the Council do provide and work a trolley vehicle system, and that a Bill be promoted in the next session of Parliament.' At a Special Council Meeting later the same day it was determined that:

> with a view to improving the facilities of communication between the districts around and the borough of Chesterfield this council approves of the establishment by the Corporation of a system of trackless trams or motor-buses: that the Tramways Committee be instructed to give the matter consideration without delay, and that they be authorised to take the necessary steps to secure Parliamentary sanction to such proposals of the nature indicated for linking up as many of the adjacent districts within the borough as they may deem advisable.

The following day several members of the Tramways Committee, plus Acland and Smith, visited Rotherham to view what was described by the *Times* of the 16th as a 'most successful installation of trackless trolley cars.' The vehicles had only been operating since 3 October, and consisted of three Railless (RET) single-deckers with David Brown chassis, Milnes-Voss twenty-eight seat rear-entrance bodies, and Siemens 20hp motors. The service was the first rural trolleybus line to run in Britain, and by courtesy of Rotherham Corporation the delegation were invited to sample the route in one of the new conveyances. Mr E. Cross, Tramway Manager, received the group and they set off along the tramline, using the overhead and a 'slipper' or skate, running in the rail groove. At the end of the rails the negative overhead arm was raised to the second wire and the journey continued. The newspaper report described how:

> The cars travelled at a high rate of speed, with great smoothness and appeared absolutely under control, while the great length of the trolley arms enabled the driver to give other traffic a wide berth, and also negotiate with ease the difficult portions of the road, which in some parts were narrow and the gradients by no means of the easiest.

The representatives noted the rural nature of the district between the termini, and concluded if the trackless was profitable in such an area, Chesterfield, with a more populous surrounding countryside, would surely benefit even more from a similar scheme. Mr Cross explained that the railless was chosen as the costs of running tramlines to Maltby would have been prohibitive; the overhead averaged £900 per mile, and each bus cost £725. He calculated that installation charges were one-fifth of tramway expenditure and, a fact the committee members appreciated only too well, tracklaying and maintenance were becoming burdensome, and their outlay much in excess of the original estimates. Trackless 'trams' were more reliable than the internal combustion engine, and they were light enough not to break up the inadequate road surfaces in use at the time. The press report ended with the view that 'today the (Chesterfield) reserve fund stands at £5,030, and the track is nearly worn out.' New feeder routes were needed to supplement the present inadequate system.

The *Times's* view on the condition of the tram rails was echoed by a correspondent the following week; he complained of 'a worn-out track and not sufficient reserve fund with which to replace it.' The nine proposed routes were listed in the same number, and powers were also sought to operate motorbuses on the same routes and also as extensions to any trolley vehicle route. Permission was also requested to test passenger traffic along any railless line by running petrol buses before investing in overhead equipment. The routes requested were:

1. From Stephenson Place to the Mansfield Road and thence to Hasland and on to the Lords' Arms at Temple Normanton.
2. From Hasland along Grassmoor Road through North Wingfield to High Street, Clay Cross.
3. From Mansfield Road, Chesterfield, along Derby Road through Winger-Worth and Tupton to Clay Cross.
4. From St Mary's Gate, Chesterfield, along Corporation Street to the Worksop main road, and along that road to the Red Lion Inn at Brimington.
5. From the Red Lion Inn at Brimington to the Market Hall at Staveley.
6. From Corporation Street, Chesterfield, through Calow to Bolsover.
7. From the tramway at the Sheffield-Newbold Road junction continuing along Newbold Road to Newbold thence along St John's Road to Sheffield Road and back to the Whittington Moor tram terminus.
8. From Whittington Moor tram terminus along Station Road and Brimington Road to Wheeldon Hill and the Red Lion Inn at Brimington.
9. From Whittington Moor tram terminus along Sheffield Road as far as the Horse and Jockey.

At a special meeting on 9 December the draft bill was approved and recommended for adoption by the council. The *Derbyshire Courier* of the 14th recorded the proposal to 'put down railless trams over nine different routes to bring the populous villages into closer touch with the town.' A Statutory meeting of the ratepayers was called for 9 January 1913, where a crowded throng assembled in the Market Hall to consider the promotion of the Chesterfield Corporation Railless Traction Bill. The Opposition, led by a former mayor, Arthur Hopkins, questioned the reliability of the relatively new trackless vehicles, but the gathering was told that capital expenditure would be much less than that needed for trams, and the viability of the routes would be initially tested by motorbuses. A section of ratepayers opposed the scheme and wished to defer it for twelve months for further consideration, and a poll was ordered on 27 January to test public opinion. Of 7,370 voters in the borough 1,291 took the trouble to record their view. 905 electors supported the bill and 383 opposed it. Three voters managed to spoil their papers. The bill thus went forward, and a Select Committee was scheduled for the following April to decide its fate.

In April the Railless Bill was presented to a Commons Select Committee and between the 15th and 30th of the month various members and employees of the Town Council, plus expert witnesses, were grilled by barristers for Derbyshire County Council and the Chesterfield Rural District Council, who both opposed the scheme, since most of the twenty-eight route miles covered by the Bill were outside the borough, in areas where the latter had responsibility for the upkeep of the roads. The Bill did not get through unscathed, and only Routes 1, 2, 4, 7 and 9 survived for trolleybus operation, though all were sanctioned for motorbus use. Despite the local news reportage of the state of the Corporation tramtrack, Acland blandly described it to the committee as in 'a very good condition' unblushingly declaring that it needed no relaying, nor any large-scale monetary outlay 'for at least ten years' – this at a time when the Whittington stretch was under heavy restoration! The Bill passed its third reading during May, and Royal Assent was finally granted on 15 August. However, due to the war, the act was never fully implemented, and cynics later suggested there had never been any intention to operate trackless vehicles along any route. The whole operation had only ever had one end – to run motorbuses on all the lines authorised. Charles Paxton Markham, a local industrialist and thrice mayor, was convinced until his dying day that there had never been the slightest aim to run trolleybuses anywhere along the feeder lines into Chesterfield, and he was not alone in this viewpoint.

Two of the most inveterate opponents of trolleybus replacement of trams were Sir Ernest Shentall (left) and Wilfred Hawksley Edmunds (right). The former, erstwhile chairman of the Tramways Committee, preferred the motorbus, while Edmunds, editor of the *Derbyshire Times*, maintained an almost incessant attack on the trackless option in the columns of his newspaper. (*Chesterfield Borough*)

# Two

# Tramway Replacement, The Battle Begins 1924-1925

At the July 1924 Tramways Committee meeting the Borough Surveyor, Vincent Smith, presented a report on the condition of the tramtrack. He pointed out that the concrete foundations were generally good, with the exception of a length between Pottery Lane and the Whittington terminus. He reminded the committee that following the recommendation of the Sheffield City Surveyor in 1919, the rail joints had all been welded, which together with sensible maintenance, had been estimated to give the line a five-year life. Smith noted that this time limit was now up, but that another four years could be squeezed out of the track if various points and crossings were replaced and broken joints cut out.

Smith also felt that there was 'a good deal of wear still left in the rails' though many of the curves were badly worn. 'In some places' he stressed 'the rim of the car wheels is touching the bottom of the groove of the rails.' In Stephenson Place track wear was so advanced that the rail tread was below the adjoining paving, and in several places crossings and points required repairs, renewals or re-packing. The final estimated bill for an end-to-end renovation of the facility was £4,000, and for a patch-up operation which would leave the line derelict in some three to four years, £2,740. After carefully considering Smith's comprehensive survey it was resolved 'That the Chief Engineer of the Birmingham Tramways be asked to present a report on the future policy to be adopted with regard to the type of vehicles to be used in Chesterfield.'

Alfred Baker was in fact the General Manager of Birmingham City Tramways, a post he had held since 1903. He had vast experience of both tram and trolleybus operation and was frequently called upon by the Ministry of Transport (MoT) to arbitrate on disputes within the industry. He was also often consulted as an advisor by other municipal undertakings, and was thus well-placed to advise on the town's future transport policy. His report was discussed at the committee meeting on the 24th. His examination of the system convinced him that the line was 'practically worn out' but with selective repairs it could endure some three or four years longer. Many rail joints were badly hammered, resulting in loose setts, damaged concrete foundations and problems with car trucks and bodies.

Baker offered only two viable options to the committee, replacement of the trams by trolleybuses or motorbuses, feeling himself that 'from the point of view of cheapness of running and ease of comfort and riding, no public service vehicle gives better results than a modern, well-designed Electric Trolley Omnibus.' Another advantage was that the power supply was municipally owned, and as customers the department would have a cheap and reliable source of electricity. 'I have no hesitation therefore', he declared, 'in advising your Corporation that it would be wise policy to abandon as early as possible your present Tramway system and in place thereof, to substitute an up-to-date system of Trolley Omnibuses.'

The report went on to consider costings for the new vehicles and equipment, and concluded that the trams would never earn sufficient revenue to pay the existing loan charges, or charges accruing for the new capital expenditure for reconstructing the service. He also felt that this applied if motorbuses were to be substituted. The only way ahead would be replacement by trolleybuses whose lower operating costs would enable the undertaking to earn sufficient income to cover all outstanding loan charges as well as the sums involved in setting up the new facility. It could be remarked that the operation of the Birmingham transport undertaking, by reason of sheer size, could better accommodate a mixture of vehicles than Chesterfield, but as a piece of special pleading the report is well worth reading. It must also be stressed that at this time motorbuses had many disadvantages, including noise, smell, low acceleration, and fluctuations in the price of petrol. The committee doubtless felt it well worth the 100 guinea fee they paid for it.

The committee meeting of 15 October was a landmark one in the history of the enterprise. As a result of Baker's labours it was resolved 'that in the opinion of this Committee the time has arrived when the tramway system should be replaced by another system of transport.' Robert Campion, the Tramways Manager, was instructed to arrange visits to Birmingham and Wolverhampton for any members who wished to see the trackless and motorbus operations in both centres. However, any consideration of future policy was hampered by the manager's resignation on the 25th to take up a position with a London power company from 30 November.

The future die was cast on 21 November, when a special Tramways meeting recommended that the existing enterprise be replaced 'by a system of trackless trolley vehicles.' A Trackless Vehicles Sub-Committee (TVSC) was appointed to carry out the resolution; its members were the chairman, Councillor Philip Moffat Robinson, the vice-chairman Alderman Sir Ernest Shentall, plus Alderman Cropper, and Councillors Barker, Moore, Syddall and Swale. Shentall was an idiosyncratic choice as he signalled his opposition to trolleybuses from the start, ploughing a lone furrow among committee members and continuing his resistance throughout the whole period leading to their introduction. There was an early check to the aspirations of the new transport policy when, on the 25th, the General Purposes Committee recommended, by an eighteen to sixteen vote, that the council disapprove the minutes relating to the railless scheme. After a full debate at the monthly Council Meeting on 2 December, the resolutions were argued and the minute advising the substitution of trolley vehicles for trams only narrowly scraped through by a close twenty-four to twenty vote. Clearly there were those in the council who were deeply opposed to the introduction of trackless traction.

Alderman Wilfred Hawksley Edmunds, editor of the town's newspaper, the *Derbyshire Times*, was definitely among the latter. Certainly the paper's editorial of that date was very hostile to the scheme, though it paid tribute to Councillor Robinson's 'very masterly speech, presented clearly and fairly' on the subject. The leader expressed the view that 'If the public are prepared to accept an engineering compromise such as trackless trolleys with their mud-splashing and skidding proclivities, and pay for them, well, there is not much more to be said.' Quite how Edmunds had come to this negative and erroneous opinion of the trolleybus is not recorded. The paper did believe however that 'the saner, better policy would have been to continue the tramways for a period, and then go for a full service of mobile buses – electric or petrol driven – one system in place of two.' This viewpoint clearly struck a chord with many people both inside the council and out, who felt the vote was too close for the enterprise to go ahead without further discussion.

Robinson now needed to gain the high ground by proving the viability of his committee's choice of the trolleybus. He was probably instrumental in persuading the Associated Equipment Company (AEC) to divert one of their vehicles on its way to Mexborough for a demonstration in town on Thursday 11 December. The trolleybus was a Brush-bodied AEC 602 single-deck thirty-six-seater with a rear entrance, the last of three ordered by the Mexborough & Swinton Tramways Co. Its despatch had been rather tardy, as its two companions had been in service since 1922! The high-set, boxy conveyance, perched on solid tyres and powered by a 33hp BTH motor, appeared in the streets of the town during the afternoon. It soon attracted the attention of the populace, who were much amused by the 'incessant sparking on the line' caused by the propulsion method, which consisted of running one trolleyboom on the positive overhead wire, with a trailing skate in the tram rail to act as a return for the current. A number of Corporation members were invited to the demonstration, and onlookers were swiftly assured that if trolleybuses were to replace the trams, vehicles 'of a better type' would be ordered for the system. It was unfortunate that no photographer thought fit to record the fleeting appearance of this novel conveyance in action during that day.

A report on the visit of the railless bus was carried in the *Times* the following Saturday, when the 'Notes by the Way' column contained the following remarks:

> Chesterfield saw a trolley 'bus on Thursday. It was a very beautiful vehicle, but its appearance does not affect the real problem. It is the system of trolley 'buses which is objected to, not the beauty or alleged comfort of the carriage of a trolley 'bus. Opposition to the trolley 'bus among Chesterfield residents is growing, and the advocates of the system will find they have a long way to go yet before they win over the whole town to their scheme. We feel that what Chesterfield ought to aim for is one system of transport – the petrol or electric bus linking up the outside districts with the centre of the town. This will not be obtained if trolley vehicles are introduced.

In the same issue Councillor Robinson put the case for the replacement programme. He listed the escalating yearly expenditure on the tramway facility, and made the rash promise that 'There will be a substantial reduction of fares the first day trolleybuses are on the road. I am certain', he declared, 'that the facts are so overwhelmingly in favour of trolleybuses that in the end reason will triumph over prejudice and doubt.' Committee members were invited to visit Keighley and Teeside on 8-9 January 1925 to inspect their railless undertakings. Charles Crossley, Deputy Tramways Manager, was authorised to distribute literature relating to the trolleybuses to council members, and it is evident that the decks were being cleared for a thoroughgoing campaign to promote the trackless cause.

A sub-committee selected six candidates for the position of manager on the 29th. The favourites were George Margrave from the Yorkshire (West Riding) Electric Tramway Co., and Walter Gray Marks from Rotherham Corporation Tramways. The former was a narrow winner, with effect from February. Crossley, in his acting capacity, submitted a report on 21 January relating to the visit to the Keighley and Teeside systems, and it was resolved that no further propaganda literature promoting trolleybuses then being exhibited in the town's tramcars and omnibuses be displayed until this report was considered. This advertising, blatantly pushed by the committee, consisted of bills extolling the capabilities of railless traction, and postcard-sized leaflets bearing the same message. Two of the larger examples have been preserved and appear in the illustrations.

At a specially called meeting on 17 March a bemused gathering were informed that after only a few weeks' service in his new position, Margrave had tendered his resignation on the offer of a seat on the board of his former employers. A new list of candidates for the post was speedily drawn up, and they were called to Chesterfield on the 27th. At the monthly Tramways meeting two days earlier there was mention of the new colour scheme for the bus fleet, with news of one example already painted in the new style. This was inspected, and the Suffield green and white shades, supplied by Kersley's of Ripon, were approved for application to all the petrol vehicles, and in due course the future railless buses.

After the interviews for the position of manager, the panel chose the candidate they should have appointed in the first place, Marks of Rotherham, who took over in April. A fifteen stone six-footer of some presence, later described as having a 'Hitler moustache' (though lacking the Fuhrer's manic temperament) he had a good pedigree in the transport industry, having risen through the ranks, and with twenty-eight years experience in electric and other traction. In the meantime Margrave had been asked, presumably to occupy his time before departing, to prepare another in the series of reports on the existing tramway and alternative methods of transport available as replacements.

A special meeting was called on 27 April to consider Margrave's recommendations on the future of the undertaking, though Marks had also been instructed to present his own ideas on the subject. These had already been discussed in draft at a meeting of the TVSC on the 4th, when it had been resolved to go for the railless choice, subject to an MOT loan, and accepting a tender from the firm of Clough, Smith. Margrave's observations and recommendations, examined twenty-three days later, centred on the four alternatives available to the committee, which included:

1. Reconstructing the present track and reconditioning the present tram fleet.
2. Laying a double tramline and reconditioning the present tram fleet.
3. Taking up the tramtrack, modifying the overhead and purchasing sixteen railless cars to replace the trams.
4. Removing the tramtrack and overhead, reinstating the road and operating omnibuses over the tram route.

Margrave discussed the pros and cons of a re-jigged tramway service, and went on to consider the trackless proposal. Following Baker, this was his favoured option, as the power supply was Corporation owned and acceleration and comfort, not to say lack of noise, were all plus factors in favour of the trolleybus. He felt too that electric traction was the only alternative which would show any surplus profit after the payment of all charges. He did suggest that if railless cars were preferred, a one-way system should be operated in the town centre, with vehicles to Whittington following the present route, but Brampton ones taking a new line via Holywell Street, St Mary's Gate, Vicar Lane and Low Pavement. All the options were costed out, with the tram estimate totalling £64,000, the trackless £40,000 and motorbuses £35,400. Further figures showed that over any one year the trolleybuses would bring in a profit of £2,100 against losses of £4,700 for trams and £3,720 for omnibuses. Margrave concluded his eighteen-page digest with the verdict that he had 'no hesitation in recommending the Committee to adopt railless traction' though he suggested that after 'earnest and careful thought' the tram service should be continued for two more years, to earn revenue to the end of its natural life.

On 16 June the same committee considered Marks' amended report, dated 12 May. The new manager wasted no time in considering alternatives, but presented a detailed scheme for tram-trolleybus replacement between Brampton and Whittington. Marks, with his experience of railless traction at Rotherham, may well have been appointed to his post as a trackless *aficionado*, and he certainly prepared a cut-and-dried plan for the changeover, publishing the tenders from eight companies for supplying fourteen vehicles, and/or the overhead conversion. Only four competed for the whole package, and Clough, Smith, offering the rewiring at £4,496 and fourteen buses at £22,092, a total of £26,558, edged out their competitors, whose bids were all more expensive. The scenario provided for the one-way town centre route proposed by Margrave, plus single wire along Stephenson Place, providing a loop into Cavendish Street for the short-working from town to Whittington.

Marks favoured Clough, Smith as he 'had previous experience of the class of material and workmanship supplied by this firm.' To the cost of the conversion would be added £10,000 for total road reinstatement, a burden they took over above and beyond the statutory duty to remove the tram rails and make good the width of the line, plus £1,000 for contingencies. After discussing the manager's report, the gathering approved the recommendations and resolved to accept the full tender of £27,548, which included the overhead equipment for the new sections, alterations to the depot, and the necessary turning circles. Application was to be made to the MoT for a Provisional Order under the 1923 Corporation Act to run trolley vehicles along the new sections of the approved route. The final estimated bill for the replacement was £38,548. Marks later wrote that four considerations induced the committee to approve the trackless option:

1. Though the capital expenditure was slightly higher than that for petrol buses, the loan repayment period was twice as long, considerably reducing the annual payments.
2. Experience from other towns showed that trolleybuses were cheaper to maintain and operate.
3. Trolleybuses could use the existing overhead and feeder cables.
4. They were more suitable for town traffic, due to the absence of smell and noise, and their acceleration enabled them to maintain higher average speeds on short routes with frequent stops than petrol buses.

It is interesting to note the 'environmentally friendly' aspect of the railless evident in the last point, though the manager would presumably not have understood the term. It deserves note in passing that the committee and sub-committee meetings during this period are out of their appropriate monthly sequence, and this may have had the effect of shortening the period of public debate before the full decisive Council meeting on 7 July. The chronology meant that both reports could be put to this meeting together, with the probable supposition that a recipe for decisive action on the matter be preferred to caution. Robinson put the options succinctly in a letter to the *Sheffield Mail* of 3 July, when he listed them as either 'wait and see' or 'do it NOW.'

In the run-up to the Council debate the *Times* kept up its pressure for a postponement of any decision to introduce railless traction, a stance which must have done much to influence opinion among the ratepayers of the borough. In later years both Marks and his successor Richard Hoggard tried to rationalise this opposition to the proposed new system. The former felt that the sharp division over trackless installation was partly due to the fact that few members of the public had ever seen a trolleybus, or understood its capabilities, having been told quite erroneously that the vehicle was prone to skidding, and was dangerous on hills in wet or icy weather. Hoggard revealed that transport managers who preached the doctrine of the trackless bus at this time were dismissed as cranks who were unleashing some sort of monstrosity on the highway, a hybrid or 'road mongrel.' Many of the self-proclaimed experts in the town were also free in their totally unfounded criticisms of the railless system, including Charles Markham, former mayor and industrialist who described them as 'gasping out their unwanted and unwelcome existence', while uninformed newspaper correspondents referred to them as 'cumbersome vehicles, unable to turn'! The only constructive comments at this time concerned the disfiguring traction poles and overhead, which would be extended along the line of the proposed one-way system. Apart from that, the strictures bore the stamp of much gossip and rumour, such as the contention that the vehicles would place an additional burden on the rates.

Philip Moffat Robinson, son of
Charles Portland Robinson, first
chairman of the Tramways
Committee, was appointed to
the same office in 1920,
relinquishing it twenty-four years
later. A great *aficionado* of the
trolleybus cause, he successfully
championed the vehicle against
supporters of the petrol bus
through several council battles
in 1925-1926. (*Chesterfield
Borough*)

Walter Gray Marks from Rotherham
Tramways was manager during the
momentous years between 1925-1929,
carrying out with great efficiency the
tram-trolleybus replacement on behalf of
his Committee. Subsequently he enjoyed
a highly successful career with both
Nottingham and Liverpool Corporations.
(*Chesterfield Borough*)

## TROLLEY BUS FACTS.

### EVERY TOWN HAS ITS OWN TRAFFIC PROBLEM.

As a general rule—

**TRAMS** are best for large cities, with large crowds to deal with and heavy peak loads.

**PETROL BUSES** are unrivalled for developing new Routes and for all districts where a frequent service is not necessary.

**TROLLEY BUSES** are best for all small Towns, where a quick and frequent service is needed, with cheap fares, but where large crowds have not to be catered for.

### TROLLEY BUSES ARE BEST FOR CHESTERFIELD.

No. 1.

---

## TROLLEY BUS FACTS.

# WHEN THE TRAMS ARE SCRAPPED

and TROLLEY 'BUSES are running
in Chesterfield:---

YOU WILL HAVE

INCREASED SAFETY,

GREATER COMFORT,

QUICKER RIDES,

LESS WAITING,

CHEAPER FARES.

This is not eye-wash---it is the plain unvarnished truth.

No. 2.

---

As part of the plan to convert the local public to trackless replacement of the tram, the Tramways Committee authorised a series of posters like the pair in the photograph, to be displayed in all Corporation vehicles. They were banned in early 1925 until reports on the future of the tramcars were presented.

# Three

# Tramway Replacement, The Battle Won 1925-1926

The vital meeting of the Town Council took place on 7 July, and lasted some $3\frac{1}{2}$ hours. Robinson and Cropper moved and seconded the motion that the minutes of the special meeting of 16 June be approved and adopted, while Councillors Haslam and Mawhood proposed an amendment that the tramways should continue for two further years. Any consideration of trackless replacement would be deferred until July 1927, when the question would again be examined. The *Times* later praised Robinson's fine speech, promoting his cause. 'He grappled a difficult situation in a clever manner' and spoke with authority and conviction. In future years opposing councillors were in no doubt that it was the Tramways Chairman who imposed trolleybuses on Chesterfield 'by the very force of his personality.' One called him 'the Joshua who had led the school of thought in favour of the trolley bus system' and Hoggard referred to 'the courageous steps' taken by Robinson in achieving his aim. In his speech the chairman recommended 'they should adopt the system for ten years and then in ten year's time they would be ready to take on what science and progress were ready to offer' – a remarkably prescient statement!

When the vote was finally taken the trackless lobby held sway, by twenty-four votes to twenty, and significantly the Mayor and nine of the eleven aldermen voted for the amendment. With the initial victory narrowly won, it was resolved to apply to the MoT for permission to run trolley vehicles in the town, and also seek sanction to open the route along the extensions previously listed. Until these had been authorised it was decided to postpone the letting of tenders for the scheme. The following Saturday the *Times* recorded its own conclusions, regretting that the council were 'committing the town to trolley vehicles which we think most hazardous in the narrow streets and which we are by no means convinced will meet the traffic problems of Chesterfield.' Nevertheless the leader appreciated that as their elected body had 'decided to take the risk of adopting trolley vehicles, there is nothing now to be done but to loyally accept the situation.' Matters were now laid to rest until the autumn, when the question of approving the route extensions in the town centre once more came up for debate.

In September the Town Clerk reported that he had applied for the Provisional Order to run trolleybuses on the routes specified by the committee. The MoT required a two-thirds vote in favour of the plan, and a Special council meeting was called to consider the matter. Not surprisingly the *Times* added its weight to the anti-trackless lobby, their 19 September issue proclaiming that 'there is very considerable feeling in the town that at all costs trolley vehicles with their poles and wires should not be allowed to invade the congested thoroughfares of St Mary's Gate and Vicar Lane.'

Forty-three council members attended the gathering on 6 October, at which Alderman Shentall condemned the Holywell Street-Low Pavement one-way system as 'a colossal blunder filling the streets with poles and wires.' Alderman Edmunds described the proposal to carry wiring round this route as 'homicide' as it was the most crowded part of the borough. Robinson reminded the assembly that the decision to direct trolleybuses along these thoroughfares had been taken by the experts called in to advise the committee, and that its adoption would ease the heavy traffic in Burlington and High Streets. It seems however that certain council members were intent on some sort of spoiling exercise as a cheap triumph to counterbalance their defeat on the general question of railless traction. They certainly opted for the worst of both worlds, as the motion, though won by twenty-three votes to eighteen, did not carry the necessary two-thirds majority to satisfy the MoT, and trolleybus traffic was duly condemned to two-way operation along the narrow through-town line established by the trams. The only part of the proposed scheme to go ahead was the loop along Holywell Street and Stephenson Place, connecting with the Cavendish Street wires for the short working to Whittington.

As ever the *Times* could be relied upon to trumpet its thoughts on the meeting. The thrust was again anti-railless, the newspaper emphasising 'we still think the adoption of the trackless trolleybus a retrograde step. No one wishes to see the town converted into a "bird cage" dominated by poles and wires simply to please these trackless enthusiasts.' Evidently the Tramways Committee had 'not yet realised the depths of feeling in Chesterfield against this trackless trolleybus proposal' and as usual, taking responsibility for their conception of the public viewpoint in the matter, the leader accused the committee of going ahead in the teeth of majority wishes. They were also accused of being more concerned with 'running after chimeras than in concentrating on giving the public what they really require.' To the columnist the council discussion 'emphasised a curious mentality on the part of the Chairman of the Tramways Committee and his closest co-adjutors. They seem to overlook the fact that they are placed in their responsible position to administer to the needs of the travelling public, and not to advance their pet theories.'

A reader's letter in the same issue revealed the usual blind prejudices about trolleybuses, and again purported to represent the general opinion of local ratepayers concerning the scheme. 'There would be a sigh of relief in Chesterfield' the correspondent began 'if the vote of the Town Council meant the end of trackless trams in the town. I never hear a good word from anyone upon the proposal to run these trolley vehicles with their network of overhead wires along our narrow streets.' He concluded with the standard nonsense about 'retrograde steps' and the necessity for 'huge open spaces' to allow the buses to turn. In fact one council member later recalled asking an objector if he knew anything about railless buses, and received a reply in the negative. 'Then why oppose them?' he asked. The response was that the man had 'read the Derbyshire Times and that had been the whole source of his knowledge of the matter'!

There is little doubt that the issue caused a schism between council members, which took much time to heal. Alderman Cropper later commented that as one of 'the infamous committee' which promoted trackless traction, they had 'possibly the greatest municipal fight in the history of Chesterfield in converting the Council and the town to the idea that railless vehicles were in the interests of the town.' A later transport manager, Richard Hoggard, also remarked on the 'very keen' battle, recording that 'there are members who fought tooth and nail against the introduction of this type of vehicle, and they still hold the same view. At the same time there are other members who fought tooth and nail for the introduction of this type of machine, and they will tell you today they have never regretted the way in which they held on to what, at that time, they considered was the best vehicle for the town they represented.'

The Tramways meeting on 14 October was informed that the MoT had consented to the substitution of trolleybuses for trams on the latter route, under the provisions of the 1923 Corporation Act. At the November gathering the TVSC was re-jigged, with Robinson, Cropper (now Mayor), Shentall, Barker, Moore, Syddall and Swale forming the membership. The MoT were asked to sanction turning circles in Stephenson Place and West Bars, which they duly did the following month.

In February 1926 members of the TVSC, plus Marks, were again on their travels, this time visiting Darlington and Hartlepool to assess public opinion on their railless undertakings. They had been preceded by a *Times* correspondent who reported on 30 January, contrasting the broad thoroughfares of the former town with the narrow confines of Chesterfield. There was also comment on the unsightly web of overhead wiring, so cluttered 'that the local wags suggest that the Council intend to roof the town as a protection against snow storms.' Marks later pointed out that the engineers, in readiness for the tram – trolleybus changeover there, had placed the trackless wiring alongside that for the tramcars, and since the reporter's visit, the latter power lines had been removed.

The subsequent TVSC report, carried by the local press on 27 February, was very heartening. Committee members travelled on the new buses incognito, asking passengers to give their opinions on the new service. A dramatic increase in travellers had apparently occurred since the changeover, all impressed with the comfort, speed and quietness of the new vehicles, though the *Times* later attempted to sour this positive view of the facility, by producing counter-claims that the citizens of the North-East were not all converts to railless traction. At the 24 March Committee meeting, Marks was authorised to survey the Thornfield Estate at Stonegravels to assess its suitability as the site for a new garage and offices. The manager had mentioned the growing unsuitability of the Chatsworth Road Depot the previous September. With the increasing motorbus fleet the locality had long been inadequate, and some buses had to be parked in the open, resulting in great difficulties in starting engines on winter mornings. The alternative options were either to build supplemental premises elsewhere and operate on a split site, or find a new locality where the whole undertaking could be re-housed. Hence the permission for Marks to check over the possibilities of the seven and a half acre premises.

The first Annual Report on the department since 1914 appeared in 1926 and showed the state of the enterprise at the end of the financial year. After all deductions the tramway side of the concern showed a bare net profit of some £93, as against £5,237 for the omnibuses. Marks recorded that 'the tramcars are not in good condition, and in view of the fact that it is your intention to scrap these vehicles at an early date, only actual work necessary for the safety of the public is executed. It has been necessary during the year to replace eight broken axles, and a considerable number of tyres which have worked loose through the hammering of bad track. The bearing shells, axle boxes, motor cases, gear cases, etc., have also suffered severely from the same cause.' Likewise the tramtrack was 'in a very unsatisfactory condition' though the overhead 'has been maintained in an efficient manner.' Nevertheless these decrepit, noisy, rattling conveyances transported 4,415,391 travellers that year, covering a record 330,104 miles along an increasingly dilapidated track. On most weekdays the average daily loading was between 10,000-12,000 riders, though Mondays were busier, with up to 14,000 passengers. On the busiest holiday weeks in June and August, numbers rose to 16,000 and 19,000 respectively. Saturdays saw the heaviest use of the facility, with some 20,000-23,000 travellers, while Sundays showed a steady 5,000-7,000 utilising the service.

A schedule of employees listed twenty-two staff and 206 other workers, including ninety drivers and seventy-six conductors. During the year £1,440 had been spent on the track, £293 on the overhead and £2,868 on the car fleet. Marks had carried out a good deal of reorganisation in the interests of efficiency, and there is no doubt that his capability and approachable manner contributed much to the increasingly favourable image of the department.

In April the Tramways Committee authorised Marks to solicit tenders for trolleybuses and overhead equipment. The results were presented on 23 June, and it was resolved to accept the bid of Clough, Smith for the whole package, at a cost of £23,947 plus £3,000 for road reinstatement and £1,000 for other contingencies. The full sum was to be covered by a loan from the MoT. A report submitted by the manager included figures showing the advantages the railless would bring, and noted that the wiring would include a reverser at Brampton terminus, as well as the three turning circles at West Bars, Stephenson Place and Whittington Moor. At the next gathering two days later it was reported that the Thornfield Estate, owned by J.E. Clayton, was for sale at the sum of £5,250, provided that the vendor could occupy the substantial house and gardens rent and rate free, for a period of five years from completion, and that the Corporation pay all conveyancing fees. The terms were approved, and Mr Clayton appears to have negotiated a very favourable deal! Further access to the estate from Hardwick Street was secured by the purchase of an area of 244 square yards for £110.

Marks had submitted a report on the suitability of the location. There were many plus factors in purchasing the estate. It was closer to the town centre, reducing the burden of dead mileage, and it adjoined the tramtrack, making it accessible to future trolley vehicles. Roads to the east and west allowed separate routes for ingress and egress, and of all the sites examined, it was the one needing least levelling. It was estimated that the full price of buying the land and building a new garage and offices would amount to some £25,639. Marks felt that concentrating all transport facilities together at one venue, plus the saving in dead mileage, would reduce the yearly operating costs by over £1,000.

There was however still one final engagement in the trackless war to be fought. Despite the *Times'* earlier exhortations that dissenting council members should 'loyally accept the situation' regarding trolleybus traction, opponents of the scheme were bent on one last spoiling operation, determined to force a vote on the minutes sanctioning the loan application for the trolley fleet and overhead, and the Thornfield Estate. The battle lines were drawn up for the 6 July Council meeting, and each side occupied their usual entrenched positions. The gathering was made more sombre by a tribute to the late Charles Markham, an inveterate opponent of the trolleybus, who died on 29 June. It was perhaps an omen. A few months earlier he had written to the local press urging that the tramway undertaking be patched up to provide a weekend service only, with a motorbus fleet covering the route during the week.

Councillor Robinson opened the ultimate trolleybus debate by pointing out that since the last discussion on the proposed replacement three more towns had opened new trackless systems, and others were in the process of changeover to electric buses. In addition, the previous Monday the MoT had announced that the government had reduced taxes on trolley vehicles to 50% of that on petrol buses, a gift to Chesterfield of £588 a year if the former were adopted. If the railless option was selected there would be no charge on the rates, but motor buses would cost 1s 8d in the pound, as they would not make enough profit to pay off the debt. The latter's lifespan was five years, and thus borrowings to pay for them had to be settled in that time. Trolleybus life was estimated as twice that of the omnibus, therefore repayments could be spread over double the period. Finally, choosing the electric vehicle was of advantage to the town as 577,000 Corporation power units were needed every year, plus 1,000 tons of local coal and a £780 contribution to the rates.

Councillor Haslam led the opposition with the predicatable emphasis on the unsightliness the scheme would involve, making 'the place hideous with its forest of poles and strings of wires in the narrow streets.' Alderman Varley counterattacked by pointing out that the whole question had been thoroughly aired over two years, and members of the committee had travelled long distances to see trolleybuses in operation. These members had approved the replacement vehicles by fourteen votes to one. Alderman Shentall, who described himself as 'the Daniel on the Tramways Committee' signalled his continued resistance to trolleybuses, which he felt would be just as much a nuisance in the main streets of the town as the trams were.

The final vote was taken, with very few members changing their rigid positions on the question. Apparently unconvinced by argument or persuasion they cast their votes very much as they had before. Only Alderman Crossley changed sides and supported the trolleybus lobby, and the final total was twenty-two for the railless preference, with sixteen against, edging up the pro vote by two on the previous one. Victory had been finally, if controversially, won.

As always the *Times* could be relied upon for a last dissenting comment. In the 10 July number the editor felt the Town Council 'are making a mistake, and there is no doubt that opinion in the town is solidly in favour of the mobile motor bus as against the trolley vehicle which is tied to a fixed route. However the majority of the Corporation have thought otherwise, and time alone will prove whether they are right.' The paper also aired its trepidation about the increased loan burden the town was shouldering, though this stance was somewhat disingenuous as this cost would be imposed whether electric or petrol buses were chosen, and the former had a ten-year redemption, as against the five years of the latter.

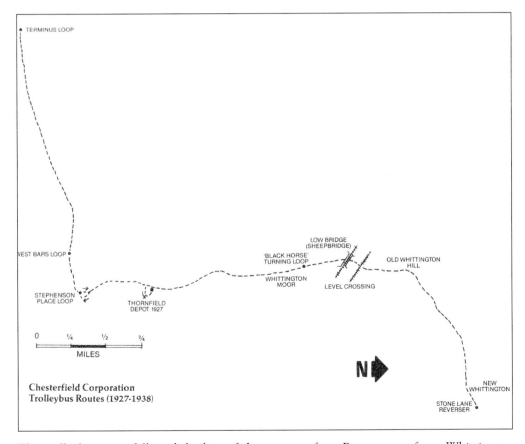

The trolleybus route followed the line of the tramway from Brampton as far as Whittington Moor. In 1929 it was extended some two miles to New Whittington, a total length of some five miles.

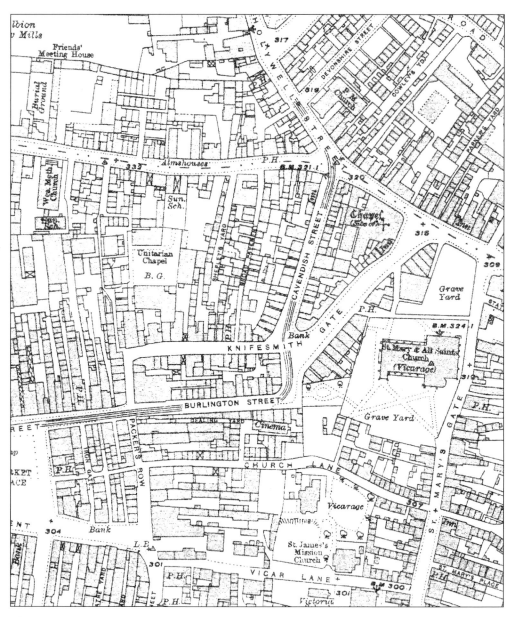

The original plan was for trolleybuses to Whittington to follow the tram route down Cavendish Street, while returning vehicles ran back to Brampton along a one-way system via Holywell Street, St Mary's Gate and Vicar Lane. Opponents in Council vetoed this scheme, and returning REVs had to utilise wires strung along Stephenson Place (shown on the map as Knifesmithgate) to connect with the main system.

# Four

# Tramway Twilight
# 1926-1927

The Tramways Department must have been fairly certain of the final verdict on the replacement programme, as plans and blueprints of the wiring modifications, the trolleybuses and the new garage and offices at Thornfield were in existence by June 1926. At the July assembly Marks submitted tenders for the Thornfield structures, including a novel steel-framed corrugated iron cladded garage from Redpath Brown costed at £7,309, brick and stone offices by Collis & Sons at £5,864 and excavating and levelling the site at £558. Work on the latter commenced on 4 August, and despite difficulties, progress was good. The main problems concerned underground streams, which caused flooding. The whole area carried underlying water channels, and a street a short distance away was named 'Sunny Springs.' One of the garage hands, Len Rhodes, recalled that the new depot had a reputation for dampness, and when wet weather fed the springs, pools of standing water often appeared on the garage floor. In fact one natural spring was later used to top up the main water tank.

At the 22 September Tramways Committee meeting it was announced that the MoT had agreed loans for the new depot and offices at £15,934, and for the new trolleybus fleet and overhead at £27,947. The gathering decided that the local firm of Reeve and Kenning would supply fourteen bodies for the electric buses, at a tender of £6,337. They were the only trackless bodies ever built by the company, though they supplied many for the motorbuses ordered by the Corporation.

At the October meeting of the Tramways Committee, members heard a report that the Straker Squire Co., from whom the trackless chassis had been ordered, were in financial difficulty, and Marks and the Town Clerk, Parker Morris, were authorised to inspect the factory and interview the receiver and the bank on the company's financial position. Having established that the contract was in no danger, the Corporation signed the agreement with Clough, Smith for the overhead and the trolleybuses on 29 October. Drawings of the single-deck vehicles showed their general design and layout and specified their electrical equipment, which was supplied by BTH of Rugby. The motors were of the BTH 508A type, giving 60hp at 500 volts, and the controllers were of the foot-operated contactor design. The overhead tender was based upon the retention of the existing pair of trolley wires, plus most of the traction poles. New heavier poles would be needed on curves and turning loops, and it was estimated that forty-two standards would need to be replaced by weightier ones. A careful examination showed that though most of the existing poles were corroded under the collars and bases, they were strong enough to support four wires on the straight portions of the route. Some sixty-eight however would need strengthening by being filled with concrete; this could be effected at a cost of £2 7s 6d per standard.

Any new posts were to be of a simple, plain design, with no ornamental scrollwork, and would be crowned with finials made of elm. The contract was exclusive of feeder cables and boxes, though it did provide for the renewal of all existing bracket arms. The 4/0 grooved positive trolley wires used by the tramcars were to be augmented by 3/0 SWG round negative wires to give two pairs of lines for the trolleybuses, plus one new pair along the Stephenson Place loop. All present span wire was to be likewise replaced by new galvanised 7/12 SWG wiring. New equipment included four No.1 poles, forty-nine No.2 and forty-seven No.3, plus finials, together with fifty bracket arms, 148 bowstring brackets, 13,325 yards of 3/0 trolley wire, and 42 cwts of 7/12 span wire. As previously mentioned, forty-two old standards were scheduled for removal, including seven made redundant by the abandonment of the Low Pavement spur.

The specifications for the new railless cars were also detailed. They featured central exits like the new Bristol motorbuses, with two saloons and a thirty-six seat capacity (later reduced to thirty-two). Illuminated destination indicators were to be fitted front and rear, plus a number indicator on the front canopy. At the November committee meeting it was revealed that the MoT had agreed, on the 9th of the month, to loan £24,947 to the Corporation, £20,498 over ten years for the new trackless fleet, and £4,449 over fifteen years for the new overhead. They also sanctioned £20,059 over forty years for the depot and offices at Thornfield. At the December assembly Marks submitted a report recommending the renewal of the existing overhead wires, presumably feeling they were inadequate for the new trolleybuses. This was agreed, and Marks received sanction to commence the work, using revenue to offset any costs not covered by the MoT loan.

Work proceeded steadily on the new site at Thornfield, though progress was hampered by the need for thorough drainage of the premises. Meanwhile arrangements were put in hand for the conversion of the Brampton section of overhead for trackless operation, the construction of the reverser at Brampton terminus, and the turning circle at West Bars. The actual rewiring commenced on 8 February 1927, but the appearance of workmen digging holes at the end of the quiet Somersall Lane for the trolleybuses to manouevre, aroused the ire of both locals and the many people who considered the quiet locality 'one of the beauty spots of the borough.' Marks received a deputation protesting about the decision to site the turn there, and promised to bring their objections to the ears of the Tramways Committee at their next assembly. The upshot was, that in the interests of good ratepayer relations, the reverser arrangement was scrapped, and three cottages at the end of Upper Moor Street, immediately west of the Terminus Hotel, were purchased for £700 to enable the department to construct a turning circle at this point. Draft byelaws were submitted to the committee at their meeting on 16 February, while the creaking tramcars ran along the Brampton section until the 28th, subjected to the end to ironic comments in the local press.

The newspapers reported on the demise of the Brampton cars, which were temporarily replaced by motorbuses from 1 March, while the overhead wiring was revamped for the trackless. It was not surprisingly the opinion of the *Times*, that had petrol buses been tried out earlier on the tram routes 'trackless trams would never have become practical politics.' The former's comfort, speed and convenience impressed all the travellers more used to the hard-riding electric cars. The sideswipe continued with the revelation that 'practically all the objections to motor buses put forward by advocates of trackless trams have proved quite mythical and the tremendous advantage of their mobility has never been sufficiently appreciated by their opponents. Meanwhile the erection of the ugly poles and wires is proceeding apace. The town is committed to the system', was the final dig, 'but we hope that motor buses will be used for all further extensions of road service.'

The same issue recorded the last week of the Brampton tram service. The final journeys on Monday 28 February passed in complete public apathy on a suitably dark and rainy day. The newspapers reported that 'the last tramcars did their last journeys almost unknown. They simply faded away in the dark and stormy night, with rain beating hard on the windows and the drivers almost hidden in their "macks." The final car from Holywell Cross, driven by Jack Rouse, with Gary Gascoigne conducting, was No.7, but Car 17 entered the depot behind it. This vehicle left Holywell Cross before 11pm, immediately before No.7, and made the ultimate journey to Brampton terminus. The latter followed on almost empty, only picking up two passengers on its way to the tramshed. It 'glided merrily along' according to a *Times* reporter who travelled on the car, hearing the conductor's final benediction of 'Good old Number Seven' as it reached base just ahead of Car 17. The newsman secured the last ticket issued on the section, a penny white numbered 89B 4251. During the day Car 7 had conveyed over 1,000 riders, completing ninety-nine miles, and it is worth recording that on that last full day the trams on service, apart from the two mentioned, included Nos 1, 2, 3, 6, 11, 13, 14 and 16. The total mileage run was 818, ferrying 13,034 members of the public.

On the following day all the open-top trams were retired from service and the Whittington line was worked with the balcony cars, Nos 6, 7, 8, 11, 12, 14, 16, 17 and 18. On the first day, and on most succeeding weekdays and Sundays, four trams operated on the shortened run, rising to eight on Saturdays. They journeyed from the depot each morning, using the positive line strung for the future trolleybuses, left live to convey them through town and on to Cavendish Street and the crossover. On 1 March Trams 8, 11, 12, and 16 were working, completing 363 miles and freighting 10,585 passengers. 2,739 car miles were recorded during the first week, as against 4,134 by the petrol buses.

The Thornfield premises were now approaching completion. The garage itself was a steel-framed corrugated iron structure, measuring 295ft by 150ft, arranged in two spans, one of 100ft, the other of 50ft. There were no stanchions in the larger bay which provided 29,500 sq.ft of floor space, clear of any obstruction, and capable of housing 100 vehicles. The smaller span contained the stores, machine, repair, body and paint shops. The offices, built by the local firm of James Collis & Sons, was a neat, modern stone-faced brick edifice, with two floors. Owing to the fairly steep slope of the site, this building, which fronted on to the main Sheffield Road, had the main door and reception area located on the upper floor which was level with the roadway. The ground floor offices were set at the level of the garage, which was some 13ft below road height. The purchase of land on Hardwick Street, which ran down the slope immediately south of the new venue, meant that vehicles could approach the depot via this route. The plan was for trolleybuses to travel down this street off Sheffield Road and enter the garage from Canal Wharf at the rear, emerging each morning from the front of the premises just behind the rear of the offices, and using the upper end of Hardwick Street to gain access to the main road. Motor buses would travel in the opposite direction, entering the depot at the front, and exiting via Canal Wharf for their journey up Hardwick Street. The garage plan and layout is shown in one of the illustrations.

One can feel great pity for the inhabitants of the once quiet Hardwick Street, especially those living on the north side, whose houses had formerly backed onto the open grounds of Thornfield House, but which now faced the huge shed rising before their eyes. Soon the revving of the omnibuses and the smell of petrol and exhaust gases would assail their nostrils, as the three fuel tanks, each holding 3,000 gallons of petrol, were sunk between the houses and the garage, and all motor vehicles filled up there every day. Noise would commence early each morning as the buses left base, and would continue until late at night. The locals did protest in September at 'the noise caused by the garaging of motor omnibuses' when the depot was fully operational, but not unnaturally the committee resolved 'that no action be taken.' Not for thirty-seven years would the residents of the surrounding streets escape the consequences of the department's decision to remove to Thornfield.

Marks' second annual report showed the continuing decline of the tramway facility. The net profit for 1926-1927 was only £30, though repairs and maintenance on the track and cars had been cut to the bone, 'having in mind the discontinuance of the Service.' The manager commented on 'the decrepit condition of the Rolling Stock and Track' and the costs involved in keeping it ticking over. While the overhead was described as being 'maintained in an efficient manner', the track was 'in a very unsatisfactory condition' as only vital patching-up had been carried out. Over the year £780 had been expended on the permanent way, £108 on the wiring and £2,724 on the tramcars. Car miles, at 290,055 were the lowest since 1922-1923, though travellers, at 4,093,900, still exceeded the four million mark.

The local press noted the arrival of the first three trolleybus chassis, over the weekend of 19-20 March, when a considerable crowd watched them being unloaded at the Market Place Railway Station. They were then towed away to the Reeve & Kenning works at Pilsley to have their bodies fitted. The Brampton town centre overhead replacement was well under way by early April. The new wiring on the system had been designed to allow railless cars to draw close in to the kerb for passenger loading, and the turning circles were wide enough to allow ample room for trolley vehicles to manoeuvre. Apart from the traction posts on straight lengths of the route, all other posts were replaced, either by medium ones on moderate curves, or special heavy examples on sharp bends or terminal loops. These hollow poles were three-eighths of an inch thick, and were set in deep concrete foundations. Wherever possible span wiring had been utilised, replacing the old bracket stanchions, but there were certain areas where bracket-arm suspension was essential, mainly through the town centre.

New brackets were fitted on these poles, with each pair of trolley wires hung from a separate bowstring, necessitating four brackets to each arm. A single bowstring weighed some 125lb, representing two 120ft lengths of 3/0 SWG round copper wire, plus fittings and insulators. The pull-offs were of a special robust design, and two lengths of clinch ears were employed, 12in ones for straight sections, and 30in ears for all curves. Two types of fittings worthy of mention were the 'CS' continuous path insulated crossings, which gave an unbroken positive or negative circuit in either direction, plus the 'CS' continuous path positive section insulators. These were helpful in maintaining speeds on gradients as they provided an uninterrupted power supply, avoiding the need to cut off current when the trolleyhead passed.

Adverse comments on the erection of the trolley standards and wires along the route continued in the columns of local newspapers. Mr Samuel Rogers, later to become a regular critic of trolleybus operation, gave an address to the Chesterfield Rotarians on 'Old Whittington' on 15 April, in which he launched a caustic attack on the appearance of the poles at the terminus. He was reported as begging the inhabitants not 'to let those misguided people who govern the transport section of the Corporation desecrate that bit of sacred soil with those needless unsightly monuments of ugliness called trolley poles, like they have done some of the best bits of architecture in the town.' He suggested that the names of the council members who voted for them should have been imprinted on them to show 'posterity who put the biggest blot on Chesterfield's escutcheon.' Rogers described the intrusive posts as 'a little array of inebriated cock-eyed poles about ten yards apart' and concluded with the observation that 'The Lord Almighty never intended man to live in a bird cage.'

The first of the new trolleybuses, No.1, was delivered to the Chatsworth Road Depot on Thursday 21 April, resplendent in its highly-polished livery of Suffield green and white. It was a square-fronted boxy looking single-decker, registration number RA 1810, bearing identity numbers on its front and rear panels, and the legend 'CHESTERFIELD CORPORATION TRAMWAYS' painted in black on the car body, above and behind the front wheels. The Corporation coat-of-arms in its customary shield appeared on one of the rear panels on either side of the body, above and in front of the rear wheels. The front compartment boasted transverse seating for thirteen passengers, including five on a long bench facing backwards behind the driver's compartment. Above this row was a bulkhead bearing two views of

Derbyshire beauty spots, and all seats were upholstered in moquette. There were two slatted wooden seats in the 4ft-wide central vestibule, set above the lockers for the bus crew. The rear (smoking) compartment had green leather-covered seats, two longitudinally fitted, and holding six riders, plus a third running across the back of the trolleybus, which seated five, making a total of thirty-two spaces. The front bay also featured luggage racks, and both were lit by frosted glass lamps. Two side windows in each bay were opened by leather straps, though with ponderous wit a reporter regretted 'they cannot be used for razor strops as they are heavily eyeletted!' 'Air Vac' roof ventilators supplemented the draught available from the opening windows. The front saloon had two windows per side, the rear one three, plus one more on the offside of the bus, lighting the central vestibule. Both saloon floors were covered with parafloor rubber, resembling linoleum but credited with a much longer life.

Each trackless car weighed over five tons, and was 26ft long, 7ft 4½in wide, and 9ft high to the top of the roof. They boasted a 14ft 6in wheelbase, and a 52ft turning circle. The lowest entrance step was 14in off the ground, and a second of the same height led into the central compartment, which was six inches lower than the two saloons, both of which were entered via a step. The enclosed driver's cab was fitted with a split sloping Triplex windscreen, and all windows were of ¼in plate glass. Access to the driver's compartment was via a single door on the nearside, and this was the only entrance to his comparatively luxurious quarters. The wheels were shod with pneumatic tyres measuring 38in x 7in, and the 60hp 500 volt motor gave a maximum speed of 25mph. The trolleybooms were superimposed one above the other on a single short mast of Estler Brothers design, the usual type fitted in earlier railless buses. The mast carried both positive and negative collectors, and could be revolved through 360 degrees. Each whippy trolleypole was 19ft long and was kept on the wire by springs supposedly capable of standing pressures of 150,000lbs, and which can be seen projecting in front of the trolleybase on contemporary photographs.

The only difference between the original blueprints for the railless and the actual vehicles was the headlamp mountings. The drawings showed them recessed into the front dash panel some half-way up, whereas they were actually mounted on either side of the base of the front end of each bus. The press reported that the trackless could be brought to a dead stop within their own length, and that emergency handbrakes supplemented the footbrake. Until 1930 the efficiency of the latter was dependent on the strength of the individual driver's foot, but electric retarders were then fitted to make braking an easier task. To train them up to their new mounts the motormen practised on Corporation motorbuses to learn the art of steering, and six drivers were sent to Rotherham to complete their tuition on that undertaking's trolleybuses. The six formed the nucleus of the group who would subsequently instruct the other staff chosen to man the new fleet.

On 22 April Straker No.1, bright in its gleaming livery, eased out of the depot and set off up to the Brampton terminus to test the electrical equipment. Though many townspeople must have noticed its almost silent passage, no one recorded the landmark on film. By the third week in May four of the trackless had arrived, and were parked in the carshed alongside the redundant members of the tram fleet. On Monday 16 May No.1 was again running, traversing the first completed section of the route between the Brampton and Market Place Station turning loops to check that all was in order for the scheduled MoT inspection three days later.

This inaugural run was something of an occasion as the TVSC, plus Marks and Crossley, were on board, and perhaps in a spirit of forgiveness a *Times* representative was allowed a seat. The trolleybus sortied at 10.45 a.m. driven by Bill Hardwick, 'spick and span in his new uniform.' At Marks' order Hardwick backed out of the shed to the accompaniment of a reluctant Bristol bus engine which someone was trying vainly to start. The pressman felt the petrol vehicle was registering an objection to the appearance of its successor on the route. The morning was dull and the road surface greasy, but the trolleybus slid easily on to Chatsworth Road as the manager pulled the bellcord, and headed east to the West Bars loop at a speed well under 20mph as Hardwick tested the manoeuvrability of his charge as it ran through the other traffic. The bus took the circle smoothly, stopping to pick up further members of the Tramways Committee, though the Mayor, Harry Cropper, was unable to make the appointment due to duties at the police court.

The inevitable crowd assembled to inspect the brand-new railless before it set off for Brampton, with Hardwick notching up the speed and moving easily past slower road users. At the Terminus Hotel the travellers disembarked, not for a celebratory drink, but to allow the sub-committee members to be photographed. On the way the smooth running of the car was highly praised; one of the councillors found he could read and write in complete comfort while No.1 was in motion. The reporter remarked that the journey from the depot to the terminus was completed in four and a half minutes. While the conveyance was halted at Brampton, one of the opposition councillors drove by and stopped his car. He even got out to study the new arrival for a few minutes, though he could not bring himself to approach the smart new single-decker, and eventually drove off. A young lady with a shopping basket was not so reticent. She climbed aboard what she obviously thought was the service bus, and was happily settling in the front saloon when an unsporting male informed her that she was on the wrong vehicle.

No.1 moved away from the Brampton loop and 'glided along again very smoothly' to the depot where the official party disembarked 'thoroughly satisfied with the first trial trip.' The full inspection of the route followed on Thursday 19 May when Lt-Col. G.L. Hall, MoT official, checked the overhead equipment between Stephenson Place and Brampton terminus, measuring the height of the wires and the diameters of the turning circles and also examining the vehicles themselves. Speed and braking tests were also carried out on the buses, and after his exhaustive scrutiny the colonel gave permission for the service to open. Six railless were ready for immediate running, but it was decided to wait to inaugurate the section on the following Monday when seven trolleybuses would be available, and the busy weekend avoided. The colonel's two and a half hour inspection was completely favourable, and he praised the single-decker involved in the checkover as 'a very excellent (sic) vehicle – quite the best he had seen.' Throughout the week the drivers were hard at work polishing up their skills on the trackless in order to attain thorough efficiency before they commenced transporting the public.

Newly delivered Straker 1, resplendent in its Suffield Green and white livery, poses at the Chatsworth Road Depot after delivery on 21 April 1927. This conveyance took part in all the early trials on the Brampton part of the system. The 4ft wide low-loading central entrance shows up well in the illustration. Note the speed limit reminder (12mph) painted on the lifeguard behind the front wheel. (H.J. Morgan)

Members of the Trackless Vehicles Sub-Committee pose in front of Straker 1 at the Brampton terminus on the official trial of this part of the route on 16 May 1927. The party includes, left to right, Councillors Barker, Swale, Syddall, Walter Marks, Philip Robinson, Councillor Moore, and Charles Crossley. (*Chesterfield Borough*)

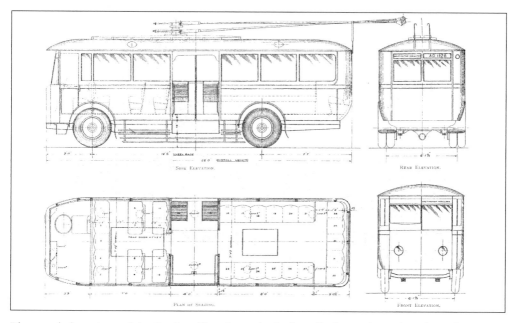

Plans and elevations of the Straker Clough single-deck trolleybuses show the salient features of the vehicles. The only modification was the removal of the headlamps from their inset position in the dash panel to either side of the base.

This shot may well have been taken on the same day as the last photograph, as the REV heads townwards from Brampton. The tramlines, seen under the bus wheels, still remain *in situ*. (*Chesterfield Transport*)

Straker 1 shown at the West Bars turning circle on the official test trials on 19 May 1927, with the Sun Inn on the left and the Market Place Station on the right. The figure in front of the bus may well be Lt-Col. G.L. Hall, of the Ministry of Transport, who was in charge of the trials. (*T. Evans*)

*Five*

# Tramway Farewell
# 23 May 1927

All preparations were now complete for the changeover from tram to trackless operation on the evening of Monday 23 May. Interestingly no trams had run at all on the first two Sundays in May, the service being maintained by petrol buses. The cars had however operated on the last two Sundays, and during the final week all the balcony tram fleet were out on the rails with the exception of Car 18, which went into retirement after Saturday 14 May. On the final day the rolling stock included Cars 7, 8, 11, 14 and 17, though the fourth tram only appeared for the ultimate official trip. The other four trams covered 310 miles, freighting 13,867 passengers. They were assisted by omnibuses on the 23rd, which ran some 167 miles.

The final act in the twenty-two and a half year history of the Corporation Tramway was played out on the dull rainy evening of the 23rd. Car 14 was selected for the final rites, despite sporting a dented dash panel and bearing the traces of its hard service, evidenced by faded and scratched paintwork. The tram had run over 24,000 miles since April 1926, and for its final appearance was in the hands of Harry Longden, former horse and electric car stalwart, and now night charge hand at the depot. The tram was due to start its journey from the Cavendish Street crossover at 7 p.m., and small groups of people began gathering as the hour approached.

A distant rumble announced the approach of No.14, which rocked around the notorious Burlington Street curve under Longden's skilful hand, its open balconies and trolleypole rather tattily bedecked with flags and bunting. One wag pointed out that at least one Union Jack was being flown in the distress position! The assemblage grew larger as the privileged guests climbed aboard, including the Mayor, Alderman Cropper, Philip Robinson, Walter Marks, all with their wives, plus most of the Tramways Committee and other council members. An appropriate touch was the invitation of ex-Chief Inspector Francis Root to join in the celebrations. Conductor C.S. Jones, smartly attired in a uniform which included highly-polished leggings and a white-topped cap, rang the bell and the loaded car pulled away on schedule, its colours flapping in a strong breeze. A policeman on Holywell Cross point duty waved the old warhorse through the junction, and all the way down Sheffield Road clusters of well-wishers cheered its progress. Conductor Jones worked his way through both decks, dispensing *gratis* green 2d tickets as souvenirs of the trip, and Mrs Cropper had the honour to receive the last one, numbered 10B 1705, which was duly autographed and dated by the Tramways Chairman. Several of these tickets, plus others issued on the first trolleybus that same night, still survive, and the local museum has examples of these mementoes.

At Whittington Moor a huge crowd greeted the arrival of the car in windy, damp weather, and welcomed the disembarkation of the committee for the statutory photograph. They included Councillor Francis Kirk, who had apparently travelled on the first, as well as the last, electric car in service. A last hurrah saw the conveyance depart on its final trip, but at Pottery Lane the car lurched and halted as a piece of rail (seven or nine inches long according to various reports) which had been broken for some time, jarred out of place and was seized by Charles Crossley. He handed it to Marks, who presented it with a flourish to Philip Robinson. The through-town rails were traversed by Car 14 for the very last time, and an even bigger gathering than that at Whittington welcomed the vehicle back to base. It came to rest on the townward side of the tramshed entrance, while on the opposite side of the road stood Straker No.1, its green and white body gleaming in contrast with the shabby two-decker in its weathered livery. Four other trackless cars were parked outside the depot, and another waited inside, ready to commence the new service.

The Tramways Committee alighted for another camera session, this time in front of the trolleybus, whose driver, the inevitable Bill Hardwick, waited in his cab. After recording the posed examples of the old and new transport the thirty-two-seater railless was boarded, while No.14 was taken home, bumping over the points as it entered the depot yard for the last time, to the accompaniment of a final accolade. Trolleybus 1 moved smoothly away from the kerb, and almost noiselessly headed down Chatsworth Road towards West Bars. The *Times* representative commented on the difference between the noisy, racketing tram and the silent progress of the trackless. The conductor was soon busy dispensing white penny tickets to the passengers. The first example was presented to Mrs Robinson, and was numbered 44C 1215. It was duly signed by the chief luminaries who were able to pen their names far more easily than in the rattling, swaying tram.

The brand-new trolleybus swept down to the Market Place, swung round the station loop and headed back up Brampton. The trip from depot back to depot took four and a half minutes, but the bus then continued towards the western terminus, picking up speed until it was travelling at something approaching its maximum of 25mph. The turning circle was easily negotiated, and once again the *prominente* offloaded for another historic photocall. The bus must have been fully freighted as extra travellers such as Harry Longden and Chief Inspector Pickering can be identified on this final official picture. Straker 1 was re-boarded and finished its duties by returning to the garage. If we can believe the press report, the sole topic of conversation was 'in eulogistic terms regarding the effective change.' No.1 had finished its duties for the day, but 2, 3, 5, 6 and 7 almost immediately commenced the short-working between Brampton and town, carrying the usual first-day *aficionados* anxious to be among the earliest to sample the novelty of the smooth-travelling single-deckers. Between them they totted up some 118 miles that evening, each bus completing twenty-one to twenty-six miles each. Councillor Robinson was doubtless well-pleased with his day of triumph and vindication, and Chesterfield seemed well set for a long period of railless transport.

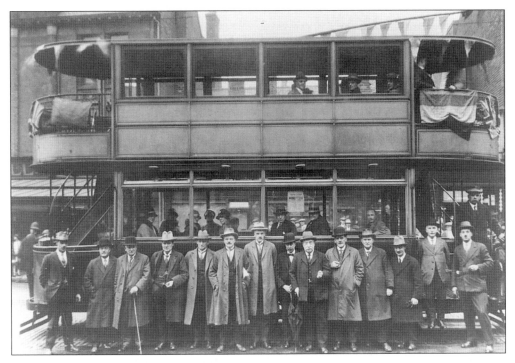

The Tramways Committee line up in a variety of natty headgear in front of Tram 14 on its final run at Whittington Moor on 23 May 1927, bunting whipped by a stiff breeze. Philip Robinson is the tall central figure, flanked on his right by the Mayor, Harry Cropper. Sir Ernest Shentall is second on his left. Marks stands extreme right, with Motorman Harry Longden behind him. (*Chesterfield Borough*)

Literally the end of the line for Car 14 as it waits outside the Chatsworth Road Depot on its usurpation by gleaming Trolleybus 1, driven by Bill Hardwick. Large crowds assembled to view the changeover and sample the new conveyances. (*Chesterfield Borough*)

Straker 1 pauses at Brampton terminus to allow for the last obligatory photograph of the disembarked *prominenti*, who include the Town Clerk, Parker Morris, posing with umbrella in front of the car entrance. Shentall, fourth from right, was presumably by this time reconciled to trackless travel! (*Local Studies Library*)

Two tickets issued on the ultimate run of Tram 14, and the inaugural trip of Trolleybus 1. The signatories include the triumvirate of Robinson, Cropper and Marks. (*Chesterfield Museum*)

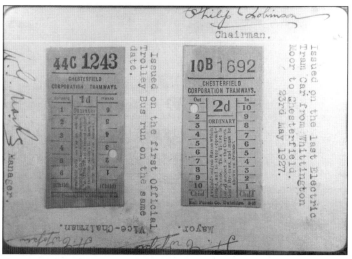

The new two-storey office block at Thornfield, which faced onto the main road. The aircraft hangar-like sliding doors of the garage can be seen behind. The author spent his formative years at 5 Hardwick Street on the extreme right of the shot. (*Chesterfield Borough*)

# Six

# Trolleybus Advent
# 1927

On Tuesday 24 May petrol buses took over the Whittington section while the overhead was converted for trackless operation, and five trolleybuses, Nos 2, 3, 5, 6 and 7, inaugurated the Brampton stretch. A few motorbuses augmented the latter, transporting 10,433 passengers on the first full day. Straker 4 did not commence service until the 28th, and the seven vehicles then delivered operated on the section until the Whittington wiring was ready on 27 July. A few modifications were subsequently carried out on the new cars, the most important of which was the conversion of the wheel bearings. They were supplied with plain phosphor-bronze bushes by the makers, but while at Thornfield these were replaced with Timken roller bearings. Usually four or five trolleybuses were on duty on weekdays, but all seven were required on Saturdays when 20,000 riders used the facility. The first week's mileage was 3,443, compared with 3,284 for the Whittington buses, but 336 omnibus miles were added to the Brampton aggregate. Until through trolleybus running commenced, the cars covered some 33,000-34,000 miles every week, supplemented by an average of 340 motorbus miles. Incidentally, throughout their service in Chesterfield the new buses were always known, for official purposes as 'REVs' (Railless Electric Vehicles), and all records and documents refer to them as such.

At the 22 June assembly the Tramways Committee undertook to bear the costs of the interest and sinking fund charges of the loan for road reconstruction, and four days later the lifting of the tramtrack was begun. This seems to have taken place at several points at the same time, and the through-town operations caused much upheaval. The *Sheffield Mail* of the 30th noted that Burlington and High Streets were closed for several days, with diversions via Glumangate and Knifesmithgate, and questions were asked as to whether it would have been better to simply tarmac over the redundant rails. The paper pointed out however that the MoT required the track to be lifted before they would contribute to the costs of road maintenance.

*Times* correspondents were swift to air their opinions on the new cars. On 2 July there were complaints that the single-deckers were quickly filled to capacity, and often passed queues of waiting travellers. On occasion several trolleybuses sailed by fully loaded, and when they did condescend to halt, fare-payers often had to stand, and then negotiate cases, boxes and even items of furniture stacked in the vestibule, when disembarking. The scribe suggested a limitation on the size of packages allowed on board the trackless, and a rescheduling of services to prevent would-be riders from having to resort to 'Shanks' Pony' to get home. As late as August the local press were complaining that 'Chesterfield today requires more buses in order to run a better local service in view of the fact that the new cars hold considerably fewer passengers than the old trams. The town service at the rush periods of the normal day is inadequate. More cars are certainly required and some speeding up of the service.' These teething troubles doubtless received the attention of Marks and his committee members.

One unanticipated problem was experienced by the growing band of wireless enthusiasts, enraged that the passage of the REVs caused interference to their reception, especially those who had the misfortune to live along the route. The local press noted at the conclusion of the trackless era the relief experienced by radio listeners at the end of the daily annoyance.

Even before the railless through-route had been opened the Tramways Committee were thinking of future developments. On 13 July they set up a sub-committee to consider new trackless and omnibus options, and to arrange for the opening of the new Thornfield premises. Fifteen days later, on the 27th, the whole system came into operation after inspection by Colonel Mount of the MoT on the 22nd. Two days previously Straker 12 came into service, followed by 11 a day later. Nos 9 and 10 joined the fleet on the first day of through running, and No.8 appeared the next day. Petrol buses actually covered more miles than the trolleybuses on the Whittington run on that first day, but they were gradually withdrawn from the 'Track' over the next week, and were henceforth only used on odd days, usually busy Saturdays. The twelve Strakers provided the full complement of vehicles until 13 August when the final two buses, Nos 13 and 14, became operational. The fourteen single-deckers bore sequential registration numbers, from RA 1810 to RA 1824, omitting RA 1818, though 13 was renumbered 15 in July 1928.

The new overhead system as completed showed some modification to the original traction pole arrangement for the trams. From Brampton terminus to the Market Place, the original twin post and span wire arrangement was retained, with special heavy poles supporting the turning loops at both ends. Bracket arms were kept through the town centre as far as Holywell Cross, where they were replaced by new poles and span wire to the Newbold-Sheffield Road junction. The new single loop line around Stephenson Place was suspended on span wire fixed to rosettes along Holywell Street as far as the right turn into the former, which necessitated the REVs pulling into the road centre to negotiate the curve. Along Stephenson Place three bracket posts took over, carrying the overhead to the turning arc where the trolleybuses could either use the frogs to proceed to Brampton, or swing right, around the façade of Deacon's Bank into Cavendish Street to engage the Whittington wires for the short weekend working. The original bracket poles remained *in situ* down Sheffield Road almost as far as Hazelhurst Lane, where new span wiring had been installed following road widening in 1923, then bracket arms took over until the Lockoford Lane junction, where further twin posts and span wires continued to Pottery Lane. According to the contemporary plans the old bracket arms then took the running wire as far as the Whittington loop, but photographic evidence suggests there was a further span wire arrangement along the final stretch. The turning circle itself, again supported by heavy stanchions, ran round a central pole of 30ft radius.

As the complete service was inaugurated some ten to twelve railless worked the route, though on Saturdays the full complement were generally out. With the opening of the whole section, serviced by a full fleet of vehicles, trolleybus miles rose to average some 8,800 to 9,400 weekly, freighting around 90,000-100,000 riders. The vehicle by-laws were published on 7 September, and contained the usual rules and regulations for operating the trackless. Mandatory clauses included the fixing of offside lights, a white one in front and a red to the rear, for use in darkness or fog. The top speed of the cars was set at 12mph, but falling to 6mph at certain points – around all turning loops, and around four curves including Holywell Street-Stephenson Place, Cavendish Street-Holywell Street, Stephenson Place-Cavendish Street and Burlington Street-

Cavendish Street. These speeds were amended two years later when the New Whittington section was opened.

During this time the Thornfield Depot had been completed and arrangements set in hand to celebrate the official opening on 27 September, though the premises had been part-occupied from 11 May. Six days before this important event the Tramways Committee gathered, operating under this title for the last time, as at this meeting they resolved to change their name henceforth to the Transport Committee. This meant that all their vehicles needed the 'TRAMWAYS' part of their logo replaced by the new wording. Arrangements were put in hand to carry out alterations to the Whittington overhead at the behest of the MoT and, as a three month trial, REVs were to be permitted to run through the town centre on Saturdays. The Routes Sub-Committee set up in July met on 13 September and put forward a resolution, sanctioned by the 1923 Corporation Act, to apply to the MoT for a Provisional Order to run trolley vehicles along eight routes within the borough. These were as follows:

1. From the Whittington terminus along Station Road and Whittington Hill to the borough boundary in High Street, New Whittington.
2. From the Whittington terminus along Sheffield Road to the borough boundary at the Brushes.
3. From the Holywell Street-Stephenson Place junction, along St Mary's Gate, Lordsmill Street and the main Derby Road to the borough boundary.
4. From West Bars along Low Pavement and Vicar Lane to St Mary's Gate.
5. From Lordsmill Street at Horns Bridge along Mansfield Road to the borough boundary.
6. From Hasland Toll Bar to the borough boundary on Grassmoor Road.
7. From the junction of Storrs Road with Chatsworth Road, along Storrs Road and Old Road to Chatsworth Road.
8. From the junction of Cross Street West with Chatsworth Road along Cross Street West to Chatsworth Road.

This comprehensive programme was due for submission to Council at a special meeting on 28 October; the delay was due to an MoT requirement for a month's notice of the gathering to be given. The resolution had to be passed by a two-thirds majority of members present and voting. Meanwhile all arrangements were in hand for the inauguration of the new garage and offices.

On Tuesday 27 September eighty guests sat down to lunch at the Station Hotel, before a fleet of special buses conveyed them to the depot where Mrs Robinson was to conduct the official opening of the garage and railless system. The gathering included many distinguished personnel including Robert Acland, the first tramway manager, T.B. Goodyer, the original tramway consultant, Alfred Baker who advised on the trolleybus substitution, plus several transport managers. Alderman Crossley, father of the deputy manager, was also present, fittingly as a representative of the last link with the old horse cars, as he was the sole surviving member of the former company. At the depot further guests joined the party, and the celebration took place in the body shop, bedecked with flags and bunting for the occasion.

The platform was decorated in green and yellow, with a display of plants from the Parks Committee. Mayor Harry Cropper presided over the programme, and all was sweetness and light in contrast with the struggles of a year ago. He asked Mrs Robinson to declare the premises open, and this was accomplished in what was patronisingly described as 'a charming little speech' after which she was presented with a bouquet of red roses. That arch-enemy of the trolleybuses, Sir Ernest Shentall, was called upon for a vote of thanks to Mrs Robinson, and the laudatory comments heralding his invitation showed that the hatchets were well and truly buried.

The party then left for a tour of the facility, being presented with copies of the well-produced souvenir brochure written by Marks, which sketched the story of the undertaking from 1879 to

1927. Special trolleybuses, probably Nos 9, 10 and 11, were then boarded to officially initiate the new electric service. The three Strakers headed for town, negotiated the Stephenson Place loop and set off for Whittington, where they rounded the terminal loop and sped back to the depot for tea. The occasion produced further toasts and speeches, including praise for Marks and Robinson. The latter wound up proceedings with a final justification for the choice of REVs for the town, though he admitted that running times were still being experimented with to produce a speedy and efficient service. He revealed that he was following in his own father's footsteps, as chairman of the committee. 'It does seem a remarkable coincidence' he stated 'that my father spent his time pulling up the rails of the old horse tramways and that I have been spending my time pulling up the rails he put down. With the march of time I hope it may be possible for my son to come and pull down the poles now erected and give Chesterfield a better system of transport.'

The visitors had ample opportunity to see how the trackless fleet were deployed in the new depot. Entering the garage from the rear, they ran to the north-east end of the premises, taking position in line-astern parallel with the wall of the building. As the depot was 295ft in length, this meant that the trolleybuses must have formed two lines, as only eleven of the 26 footers could have been accommodated in single file. No plans survive of the wiring arrangements for trackless access on to Sheffield Road, and fading memory must be relied on. According to old employees overhead wires connected with the main Chesterfield lines via a left turn, and the Whittington ones to the right, both activated by a system of frogs. The Strakers turned back down Hardwick Street to the depot by pulling up before the turn from either direction and swinging over the trolleybooms to the opposite overhead to enable them to return home, an operation feasible enough in those days of comparatively low traffic density.

Aerial view of the new transport premises at Thornfield, with a motorbus filling up at the petrol pumps. Trolleybuses travelled down Hardwick Street on the right, entering the premises from the rear. They emerged through the front along the access road behind the offices fronting Sheffield Road. Thornfield House, later the transport manager's home, can be seen at the top left. (*Chesterfield Transport*)

Schematic plan showing the routes taken by the REVs and motorbuses as they entered and left the Thornfield premises.

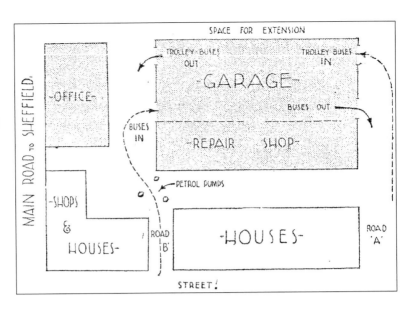

A view of the front (non-smoking) compartment of Straker 5 taken from the central vestibule. The saloon, seats upholstered in green moquette, seated thirteen passengers. An additional two wooden seats were available, bottom right, in the central section itself. Note the two Derbyshire scenes above the front bulkhead. (*Chesterfield Transport*)

The rear (smoking) compartment of the same vehicle. Here the seating, covered in green leather, ran the length of the trolley, and across the rear, providing accommodation for seventeen riders. (*Chesterfield Transport*)

Trolleybus 12 parades its boxy lines at Brampton terminus in the first summer of service. The photograph shows the turning loop and the still-existing tramlines. On the right is a solitary milk cart, and the two lodges originally on either side of the road leading to Somersall Hall. (*Chesterfield Transport*)

A superb study of Straker 4 in sylvan surroundings on West Bars in summer 1927. The tramlines still linger, and the Estler trolley housings and long booms show up well in the shot. The plaque on the lifeguard gives the kerbside weights and dimensions of the REV. (*Chesterfield Transport*)

Trackless 7 demonstrates its flexibility as it eases past a sporty-looking Vauxhall open-topper on Burlington Street, another 1927 photograph demonstrating the ability of the trolleybuses to negotiate other traffic in busy urban situations, one great advantage over the tramcar. (*Chesterfield Transport*)

At Whittington Moor a lightly passengered Straker 1 negotiates the 30ft radius turning loop for the journey back to town. (*Local Studies Library*)

A rather fuller freighted No.10 on the same loop in 1927, two years before the electrification of the New Whittington section. The complicated wiring of the circle shows up well in this shot, with the supporting 'pull-offs' visible on the right. (*Chesterfield Transport*)

Another nearside view of Straker 3 at Brampton terminus, in front of the inn of the same name. Note the smart martial style of uniform then in vogue – 'maternity' type jackets, tailored riding breeches and polished leggings. Two of the drivers have been tentatively identified, Briggs on the left and Cutts second from right.

# Seven

# Wires through Whittington 1927-1929

The Transport Committee assembly on 12 October was fairly routine, though it contained a protest from a body calling itself the New Whittington Tradespeoples' Association, who were against the proposed railless penetration into their locality. 'No action was taken thereon' though letters to the *Times* supported the extension, denigrating the 'narrowed point of view' and 'rank impudence' of the tradesmen, and those representing the Whittington Moor Chamber of Trade, who also opposed the plan, though for different reasons. Most travellers to the former destination were galled at the need to change from trackless to omnibus at the Moor. There was no through running because this would involve duplication, and petrol buses only provided a feeder service from the Whittington Moor loop to New Whittington. A through electric bus route would enable passengers to shop more cheaply in Chesterfield and avoid the higher-priced goods vended at the smaller suburban outlets.

On 25 October, the full Council, attended by thirty-eight members, discussed the proposals for the new trackless routes drawn up by the Transport sub-committee in September. The list embodied the whole railless programme scheduled for promulgation over the next three years, and as such was a blueprint for their intentions. It is clear however that their immediate objective was to implement the New Whittington extension plan as soon as possible, and use that as a test-bed to gauge whether its success would encourage the council to consider the other routes in due course. The next few years would see if the town was to pursue a committed railless policy or opt for expansion via the motorbus. Philip Robinson outlined the rationale behind the extension plans, and noted that despite the restraints caused by the lifting of the tramtrack, passenger traffic on the trolleybuses had increased by up to 15% since their introduction. This had encouraged the committee to consider opening up new routes. The pros and cons of the propositions were discussed for an hour, prompting the usual dissentients, supporters and advocates of the 'wait-and-see' policy. Sir Ernest Shentall was in his usual opposition mode, parroting his familiar 'hideous and disfiguring network of poles and wires' theme, and the inflexible nature of the electric bus, firmly tied to its overhead. Violet Markham supported the extension of the linear route to New Whittington as a logical step, but was 'not anxious to see the town covered with wires or poles where they could be avoided.' Councillor Swale, obviously pre-primed, proposed that this first line be promoted, and the others set aside for future consideration. Robinson speedily agreed, and the resolution was carried 'by an overwhelming majority.'

Alderman Shentall tried to postpone consideration of the extension for twelve months, citing the spurious notion that trolley vehicles would have difficulty in negotiating Whittington Hill in icy or snowy weather, but his amendment was brusquely squashed. Robinson labelled him the 'Apostle of waiting' suggesting that he would still have been running the tramcars had he been in charge of policy, and that the hill could cause difficulties for buses once in five or six years. The final vote, needing a two-thirds majority for adoption, resulted in a thirty to eight victory for the trackless lobby, and it was immediately resolved to apply for a Provisional Order authorising the Corporation to use railless vehicles on a continuation of the Whittington stretch to the borough boundary in High Street, New Whittington.

Though there is no doubt that the majority of residents of this outlying community would have welcomed any type of through transport, the decision to inaugurate trolleybuses did have its local objectors, including that familiar anti-trackless agitator, Mr Samuel Thomas Rogers, who was standing as a councillor for Old Whittington Ward, and who was obviously stirring up criticism as a parish pump ploy. At a local meeting on the night following the council decision he gave vent to some scathing remarks on the proposal, attacking the junketings at the opening of the new depot, and amusing the enthusiastic gathering by his protests. He even insisted that one member of the Transport Committee had personally threatened 'We are going to make you have (trolleybuses) whether you want them or not.' It was good knockabout stuff and certainly enlivened the occasion in question.

Meanwhile the trolley fleet maintained its early promise, achieving a high standard of serviceability and enabling the manager to wean the petrol buses off the route almost completely. In February 1928 the committee were informed that the total overhead conversion amounted to £5,794, an overshoot of £545 on the original estimate. On the 15th of the month a public enquiry was opened to consider the Corporation's application to extend the railless service to New Whittington. According to the *Times*, Parker Morris, the Town Clerk who conducted the council's case, 'had a sound if not strong hand, and played his cards to a nicety.' He pointed out that the trackless extension would dovetail into the existing route with no duplication of services, and no extra expense. 'There is no alternative' he said 'it is either a through trolley route or Whittington must do without its through route. It is the definite considered opinion of the Corporation.'

Most of the varied objections were fairly petty and were easily deflected. Apart from the old chestnut that the local railless system had not been tested enough, and that parts of the intended route were dangerously narrow or steep, the most serious query was whether the proposal would increase the rates or run at a loss. Robinson assured the meeting that 'Chesterfield ratepayers had never been called upon to pay one penny on the rates for transport facilities from the day the first tram ran in the town.' In fact the Transport Committee, in addition to contributing to rate relief, had paid the charges for road reinstatement after the lifting of the tram rails. As for the prospects of losing revenue, he affirmed 'We shall make a substantial profit from the first day we run the trolley service.' With no competition from other bus companies, this was a fairly safe bet.

Figures showed that profits on the railless route were rising, and vehicle costs falling since the inauguration of the new transport undertaking. The following day the objectors made a final effort to influence the MoT Inspector, A.D. Erskine. W.F. Donald, representing the property owners, made an impassioned plea that 'we ought not to be offered up on the altar of Councillor Robinson's ambition' calling the latter 'the Joshua who had led the school of thought in favour of the trolley bus system.' Marks countered the objection to the extension by revealing that 32% of travellers to and from New Whittington had to break their journey at Whittington Moor, and many of them had asked for a through service. Henry Williamson, General Manager of Bradford tramways, retained as an expert at a fee of 50 guineas, confirmed that REVs were the most suitable vehicles for the service, due to their economy and efficiency.

For the railway companies who objected both as competitors and ratepayers, Mr Hope made the fatuous claim that 'the trolley system had failed everywhere, and might fail in Chesterfield.' Colonel Sinnot, Surveyor for Gloucester County Council, felt the route to be unsuitable for railless cars, while Mr Herbert Needham managed to contradict himself by assuring the gathering that the local inhabitants felt there was no demand for trolleybuses, yet in the next breath complained of long waits for transport at Whittington under the present traffic arrangements! There were also protests that 'the erection of standards was an eyesore, and it was an absolute desecration to erect poles in Old Whittington.' The aforementioned Mr Donald felt 'the trolley system had been imposed upon Chesterfield by the very force of (Robinson's) personality' and that the decision to proceed would be 'a leap in the dark.'

Inspector Erskine departed to consider his decision at the close of an enquiry described by the local press as 'undertaken with remarkable thoroughness.' The *Times* noted the opposition to the scheme and questioned whether any demand for the facility 'existed in fiction or fact.' Robinson had been portrayed, somewhat unconvincingly as 'a municipal Mussolini' but the main questions hinged on the likely prospects for the route and the validity of the opponents' arguments. 'It is to be hoped' was the final comment 'that Coun. Robinson's expressed desire that the system most satisfactory to the largest number of ratepayers may be adopted, will be reflected in the Ministry's finding.' A few months wait now ensued while the MoT weighed its verdict.

The final traceable pre-war Annual Report on the enterprise covers the period 1 April 1927 to 31 March 1928. The department continued its growth, and there were now 23 office staff and 234 other employees, including 106 drivers and 79 conductors. The fourteen Strakers had clocked up 338,681 miles since 23 May; the biggest mileage had been run by No.7, which had completed 28,386 miles, the smallest by No.14 with 20,092. 4,060,445 passengers had been freighted, though these included riders carried on the motorbuses augmenting the railless on both main routes. Initial repairs and maintenance had been heavy, with £463 expended on the overhead, £1,319 on the vehicles, and, a new item, £1,354 on tyres. Traffic receipts included £23,519 for travellers, £10 on advertising, and £42 on parcels.

A fares schedule survives from this period. It shows that the two sections were divided up into five fare stages, with prices as follows:

BRAMPTON SECTION

|  | Fare stage | Barker Lane | Heaton Street | Brampton |
|---|---|---|---|---|
| Stephenson Place | 1 | 1d | 1½ | 2d |
| Foljambe Road | 2 | | 2d | 1½d |
| Barker Lane | 3 | | | 1d |
| Heaton Street | 4 | | | 1d |
| Brampton Terminus | 5 | | | - |

WHITTINGTON SECTION

|  | Fare stage | Hare and Hounds | Nelson Street | Whittington |
|---|---|---|---|---|
| Market Place | 1 | 1d | 1½d | 2d |
| Albert Street | 2 | | 1d | 1½d |
| Hare and Hounds /Nelson St. | 3/4 | | | 1d |
| Whittington Moor | 5 | | | - |

WORKMEN

BRAMPTON SECTION

| | |
|---|---|
| Chesterfield-Heaton Street | $1d$ |
| Foljambe Road-Brampton | $1d$ |
| Chesterfield-Brampton | $1\frac{1}{2}d$ |

WHITTINGTON SECTION

| | Fare stage | Nelson Street | Whittington |
|---|---|---|---|
| Chesterfield | 1 | $1d$ | $1\frac{1}{2}d$ |
| Albert Street | 2 | | $1d$ |
| Hare and Hounds /Nelson St. | 3 | | $1d$ |
| Whittington Moor | 4 | | - |

Workmens' fares operated until 9 a.m. from both termini.

At the 16 May meeting of the committee the Town Clerk reported that the MoT had submitted a Parliamentary Bill to confirm the Order for the trolleybus extension to New Whittington, and that the manager was authorised to advertise for tenders for the necessary work. On Saturday 16 June the Chesterfield public were intrigued by the appearance of a 'big blue trolleybus' which ran 106 miles on that date, and seventy-three the following Tuesday. Enquiries revealed that the central-entrance single-decker was built by the English Electric Co., and was on a fleeting demonstration visit to the town. It was previously thought that only the Leyland Co. ran demonstrators in the borough, but the EE vehicle, built in 1927 as a thirty-one-seat rear-entrance bus, was redesigned with a mid-entrance for faster loading, and paid a brief visit to Chesterfield, perhaps on its way to Maidstone. The trolleybus had rheostatic brakes fitted as well as normal foot and hand brakes, the first saving wear and tear on the ordinary system by operating on the back axle and producing a retarding effect on the rotary motion of the motor. Unfortunately no photographs of this singular visitor under local wires have so far surfaced. It apparently carried the registration plate CK 3898.

New uniforms ordered for the department in June 1928 favoured a marked military style, with 'maternity' type jackets and tight riding breeches similar to those affected by officers of the German armed forces. Supplemented by polished leggings and smart peaked caps, the bus crews' outfits exuded a distinctly martial air. On the 16th of this month Straker 13 ran for the last time bearing its original number. The reasons for the change emerged via the *Times* in its issue of the 28th, when it was revealed that though 'Town Councillors and other wise people are notoriously unsuperstitious, the same cannot be said of all Corporation employees.' The barb was aimed at the trolleybus crews who had persuaded themselves that RA 1823 was an unlucky vehicle. Apparently 'the trolley poles came off the wires; if there were any delays bus 13 was sure to be involved; and all the people who habitually disregarded notices and jump on and off moving cars were either cut or bruised in the process. Drivers and conductors dreaded their duty on bus 13.'

The outcome was inevitable. 'No magic spell was breathed. There was no salt carried on the bus. It was just this; bus 13 went to bed in the depot as bus 13. In the dead of night someone changed the number! It is now bus 15 – and in case any particle of ill-luck clings to it, a first-aid outfit has been placed in the centre compartment.' Straker 15 first ran with its new designation on 19 July. Strangely there was no comment on the fact that Tramcar 13 had run happily for some twenty years with no suggestion that its fleet number was unlucky.

On 18 July the Transport Committee accepted the tender of F. Mason and Co. for a five year contract covering sole advertising rights on the whole bus fleet, costed at £1,000 per annum. Some, but not all, of the Strakers had boards fixed along the roof line to carry the details of the offerings of various firms. Examples identified include the Sheffield Furniture and Exchange Co., Ediswan light bulbs and ROP (Russian Oil Products). In November the same company secured the advertising rights on tickets at a price of £6 5s per million. It was also resolved to accept the offer of British Insulated Cables (BIC) to supply and erect the poles and running wire for the New Whittington extension.

The Chesterfield Corporation (Trolley Vehicles) Order Confirmation Act 1928 was passed on 3 August, and sent to the Town Clerk who reported its arrival at the 19 September gathering of the committee. In the meantime the Highways Committee had inspected the new route with the aid of Marks' plan, and approved the positioning of the new REV standards as long as poles 66 to 68 were set back to the boundary wall of the highway. On 17 October the members of the Transport Committee resolved that the trolleybus system be extended to New Whittington, operated by electric buses on every day but Saturday when motorbuses would supplement the service. Application was to be made to the MoT to borrow £4,700 and BIC were to be granted the contract for the poles and wiring at a total cost of £5,042.

The augmentation of the trackless route was debated at a Special Council meeting on 3 October, and was attended by forty-one members. By now Robinson must have known he was on the home straight, and that the proposal would be approved by a large margin, despite the presence of the usual irritants such as Shentall and the local dissident, now Councillor Rogers. True to form, the Alderman called the scheme, in terms he had used more than once before, 'the biggest blunder the Transport Committee have ever made.' As befitted the fairly new member for Whittington, Rogers was vociferous in his own condemnation of the project, with its 'beastly, rusty poles' disfiguring the streets, and railing against 'hundreds of rusty poles with wire netting over them.' He amused himself, and doubtless the gathering, by recounting the tale of a trolleybus which left town at 10.30 p.m. the previous winter in thick fog. At Dark Lane its 'duck' came off, killing the lights and making it impossible in the darkness and dense vapour to fit the trolleybooms back on the invisible wires. An inspector located the immobile vehicle and persuaded some half-dozen stalwart passengers to push it round to Nelson Street where they were able to re-engage the poles on the overhead. The Straker reached Whittington Moor at 11 p.m., too late to link up with the last motorbus to New Whittington. No one pointed out to Councillor Rogers after this entertaining if obtuse ramble, that had the wiring then been in position the REV could have continued its progress to the far terminus with no need of any connecting transport! The only other point raised was a complaint at the slowness of the trolleybuses, a theme raised more than once over the years. 'Why should we be condemned to this funeral hearse type of transport?' was the question asked. The MoT should have been the body answering the query, as it was they who had fixed the speed limit at 12mph.

The final vote was overwhelmingly in favour of the extension. Robinson, who was elected Mayor in November, had won the final round in the trolleybus wars. He was soon to lose his Transport Manager, as Marks tendered his resignation on the 21st on his appointment as manager of Nottingham City Transport with effect from 1 January 1929. The Transport Committee put on record 'its appreciation of the services rendered to the Borough, and wished him every success in his new appointment.' Walter Marks went on to great things in the industry. His tenure at Chesterfield had been a highly successful one, and he would be a hard act to follow.

Marks' post was swiftly advertised, and six candidates were chosen from the forty-eight who applied. Richard Hoggard was appointed to the post after a selection meeting on 30 November. He was a forty-eight-year-old Sheffielder who had worked for the tramways of his native city for twenty years. He had subsequently been appointed to a post at Lincoln, and had taken Marks to the wire at Nottingham, as he and the latter had been the final two candidates for that position. He duly took up his new duties on 1 February 1929.

The MoT sanctioned the loan of £4,700, over twenty years, for the equipment for the extended service, and BIC sent their tender for the work. The schedule gave the length of the new working as 9,390ft, requiring fifty-five medium poles for span wiring, sixty-two medium poles with 16ft bracket arms, and five heavy poles for pull-off positions. 12,250yds of 3/0 grooved copper trolley wire were necessary, and the layout of the Whittington Moor loop had to be modified to allow a run-off for vehicles turning into Station Road, and wiring for buses returning along this highway towards town, again via a connection with this same circle. With two heavy standards and six medium ones, plus 950ft of running wire, frogs, ears, pull-offs, insulators, etc., the cost of the altered junction was estimated at £213.

Since there was no room for a turning circle on High Street, New Whittington, a reverser was planned at Stone Lane. This needed eight heavy and two medium stanchions, plus 1,200ft of wire and all the fittings, supplied and erected for £258. Trolleybuses would pull ahead of the entrance, then back into the 'turning triangle' where the automatic frogs would guide the booms onto the opposite wires. Other necessary material included 80ft of wooden troughing between poles 7 and 8 for the overhead to pass under the 14ft 10in low bridge carrying the Midland Railway over Station Road. The whole cost was estimated at £3,274, and operations commenced on the new overhead later in the New Year; the work was completed in some three months. Transport Department blueprints show that the overhead was carried on bracket arms from the Whittington loop to the bridge at Sheepbridge station (poles 1 to 8), followed by span wiring to Whittington Hill (poles 9 to 24), then almost continuous bracket arm wiring to the New Whittington reverser (pole 101), apart from a short stretch of span wire between poles 61 and 71.

The end of March figures show that the Strakers had covered over 460,000 miles during the year, carrying 4,968,062 passengers. The mileage clocked up by each bus was remarkably similar, with all vehicles covering between 31,000 and 35,000 miles. Hardest worked was REV 11, which recorded 34,696 miles. No.9 had the lowest figure with 31,234. Repairs and maintenance came out at £593 for the overhead, £1,379 for the trolleybuses and £1,495 for the tyres, which were reckoned to be good for 28,000 miles each on the trackless. Gross passenger receipts were £28,267, with £36 profits on parcels and £51 on advertising. In April the Chesterfield Postmaster sought permission to place collection boxes on various route vehicles, including the 8.30 p.m. railless from New Whittington. The request was agreed, subject to a fee of 30s per annum per box, and the GPO to provide the boxes in question.

It would seem that the construction of the poles and overhead began at New Whittington and moved inward towards town. Just north of the bridge at Sheepbridge was a level crossing, carrying a branch line. It has been reported that trolleybuses travelling at too high a speed over the tracks could bounce their booms off the running wire! Immediately south of the crossing a section box fed 'juice' into the overhead at 600 volts to boost the power for the steep climb up Whittington Hill. Sometime during the month the department received a deputation from Essen, led by the Burgomaster, who were given a tour of the facilities, an event which seems to have escaped the notice of the local newspapers.

On Thursday 25 July the extension was inspected and it was decided to open the new system the following Monday. Members of the committee, plus the council, were invited to look over the route by trolleybus, and were then taken to Walton Road where they boarded a motorbus which took them to the new transformer station. On the Monday all the Strakers except No.2 were out on the railless route, completing 1,576 miles. A timetable issued by the department at this time is illustrated, and shows the New Whittington timings and fares. These timings show the average number of minutes taken to travel each section of the route. The journey from Brampton to Stephenson Place took ten minutes, from thence to Whittington Moor fourteen minutes, plus a further fifteen minutes to New Whittington, allowing forty minutes for the through run.

The opening received no cover in the local press, apart from another enjoyable rant by the inevitable Councillor Rogers at the Tuesday the 30th Council meeting. He gave vent to a lengthened tirade as he bemoaned the total lack of interest displayed by the Corporation in the affairs of his locality. 'Look at High Street, Whittington today' he lamented 'the Transport department have put up the worst bit of tramway engineering in the whole of the British Isles. The poles have got rheumatism already and have to be tied with bits of wire, cross stays, crutches and guy ropes, and they look more like the gallows of a Punch and Judy show than an engineering job. The top of the poles are festooned with overhead feeder cables like dilapidated clothes lines.' He continued his outburst by describing the passage of the first Straker into his domain. 'The very first official trolleybus with the Mayor and Corporation in it', he declared, 'tried to get away from such a scene. It did get its duck off, but owing to the weight of officialdom it couldn't get away. Somebody with no more feeling for the trolleybus than the Big Five of the Improvements Committee have for Whittington, stuck its duck on again, and it is now condemned to spend its life like Whittington people, in passing daily the most abominable and disgraceful piece of street decoration the mind of man could devise.' Presumably the Council members relished these periodic exhalations of Sam Rogers, adding as they did, spice to the more humdrum business of local administration.

On Saturday 16 June 1928 a 'big blue trolleybus' appeared on the Chesterfield streets. The vehicle, an English Electric demonstrator, completed 179 miles on the route, and probably paid its short visit on its way to Maidstone. (*Chesterfield Transport*)

Straker 6 halts at the Whittington terminus some time in the first two years of the service, utilising the loop to return to town. New Whittington passengers caught the motorbus seen at the stop by the Black Horse Inn. The running wire looks a little slack in this view. *(A. Bower)*

Straker 15 bears down silently on an unsuspecting motorcyclist on a quiet Sunday High Street on 5 August 1928. Less than a month earlier this particular vehicle was numbered 13, but superstitious crews apparently forced the change on 17 July. *(Local Studies Library)*

*Above:* Straker 6 heads Brampton-wards through an almost deserted New Square in 1929. Note the feeder box on the right, providing power to the cables supplying the overhead above. (*Local Studies Library*)

*Right:* The railless extension to New Whittington was constructed in 1929, and the route was opened on Monday 29 July. The plate shows the new timetable and fares on the facility. Despite high future hopes, this was the only electric bus augmentation to be implemented.

---

**CHESTERFIELD CORPORATION TRANSPORT DEPARTMENT.**

# NEW WHITTINGTON EXTENSION

### Trolley 'Bus Service will commence on Monday, July 29.

Trolley 'Buses leave **Brampton Terminus** for **New Whittington**
at 6-36 a.m., 7-9 a.m., 7-39 a.m., and every half-hour until 2-39 p.m. then every fifteen minutes until 10-9 p.m.   Last 'Bus 10-21 p.m.

Trolley 'Buses leave **Stephenson Place** for **New Whittington**
at 6-46 a.m., 7-19 a.m., 7-49 a.m., and every half-hour until 2-49 p.m. then every fifteen minutes until 10-20 p.m.   Last 'Bus 10-30 p.m.

Trolley 'Buses leave **Whittington Moor** for **New Whittington**
at 7-0 a.m. and every half-hour until 3-0 p.m.   Last 'Bus 10-30 p.m.

Trolley 'Buses leave **New Whittington** for **Chesterfield**
at 7-15 a.m. and every half-hour until 3-15 p.m. then every fifteen minutes until 10-45 p.m.   Last 'Bus from New Whittington at 11-0 p.m. to Depot only.

#### FARES.

| | NO RETURN FARES. | | | | | WORKMEN. | | | | |
|---|---|---|---|---|---|---|---|---|---|---|
| | HARE and HOUNDS. | NELSON STREET. | WHITTINGTON MOOR. | COCK and MAGPIE. | BRIERLEY STREET. | NEW WHITTINGTON. | NELSON STREET. | WHITTINGTON MOOR. | COCK and MAGPIE. | BRIERLEY STREET. | NEW WHITTINGTON. |
| CHESTERFIELD     TO | 1 | 1½ | 2 | 3 | 3½ | 4 | 1 | 1½ | 2½ | 3 | 3½ |
| HARE AND HOUNDS   „ | — | 1 | 1 | 2 | 3 | 3 | 1 | 1 | 1½ | 2½ | 2½ |
| NELSON STREET   „ | — | — | 1 | 2 | 2½ | 3 | — | 1 | 1½ | 2 | 2½ |
| WHITTINGTON MOOR   „ | — | — | — | 1 | 1½ | 2 | — | — | 1 | 1 | 1½ |
| COCK AND MAGPIE   „ | — | — | — | — | 1 | 1½ | — | — | — | 1 | 1 |
| BRIERLEY STREET   „ | — | — | — | — | — | 1 | — | — | — | — | 1 |
| NEW WHITTINGTON   „ | — | — | — | — | — | — | — | — | — | — | — |

WORKMEN'S FARES WILL OPERATE UP TO 9-0 a.m.

TRANSPORT DEPT.,
CHESTERFIELD (Tel. 2357),
24th JULY, 1929.

R. HOGGARD, M.Inst.T.,
General Manager.

*Above:* Soon after the New Whittington extension was opened, Straker 2 transported local photographer Tommy Evans to record the workings of the Stone Lane reverser. Here the REV waits at the LMS level crossing at the foot of Whittington Hill. The feeder cables, boosting the power to the overhead for the steep climb, can be clearly seen. *(T. Evans)*

*Left:* Straker 2, here shown with advertising boards, manoeuvres into position to back into Stone Lane for the return journey to town. *(Chesterfield Transport)*

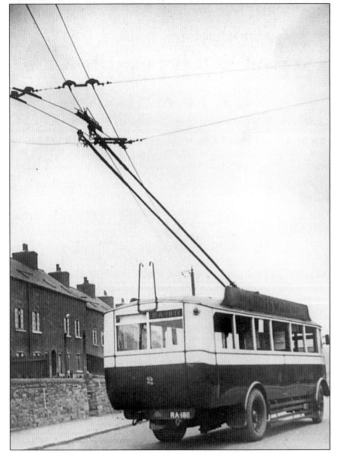

*Above:* A rear view of the trolleybus looking across High Street and down Wellington Street opposite. The wiring details of the 'turning triangle' show up well. The houses on the left have been replaced by modern bungalows. *(Chesterfield Transport)*

*Right:* Booms in position for the return journey, REV 2 waits at the terminus, then a fairly undeveloped locality. Again the reverser wiring arrangement is well displayed in the plate. *(Chesterfield Transport)*

# Eight

# The Later Years
# 1929-1937

The new service seems to have amalgamated itself smoothly enough, though the Saturday petrol bus miles increased, as it was always intended that these vehicles would supplement the trackless on this day. By the end of March 1930 motorbuses had totted up some 30,000 miles on the trolleybus route. The mileage book reveals that Woolworth's new store opened on Saturday the 28th, and on that day extra services were run to cope with the eager shoppers.

On 19 September the amended trolleybus regulations and byelaws were published, revising the earlier ones and embodying the rules for the new extension. The vehicles now had to exhibit two frontal white lights, and a red rear light in darkness or fog. The speeds of the REVs were changed to allow a rate of 16mph along most of Chatsworth and Sheffield Roads, except while descending Stonegravels Hill when a 12mph limit was imposed. There was an 8mph restriction on the Whittington Hill descent, and on High Street, New Whittington, between Broomhill Road and Twelves Corner (pole 425), and between Handley Road and the reverser. The 4mph limit had an addition for the short stretch under the LMS low bridge on Station Road on the new part of the route. At all other places the speed was set at 12mph. Two mandatory stops were also specified, on High Street, New Whittington, at pole 464 near the junction of Handley Road, and on Whittington Hill at pole 391 near Prospect Road, again on the descent.

At the October gathering, Berresford and Blanksby were awarded the contract for painting 365 traction poles in dark green, evidently the usual colour. There was some interesting correspondence in the Sheffield press in November, relating to the town's electric transport. One communicant to the *Telegraph and Star* on the 20th, praised the Chesterfield traffic system, comparing the smoothness and quietness of the REVs with the noise of the city's tramcars. There was a rejoinder on the 28th from a 'Trolley Bus User' who disputed the first writer's conclusions. 'It requires a long stretch of imagination' he wrote 'to compare Chesterfield's trolleybuses with Sheffield's tramcars. (He) ought to be at one of Chesterfield's stopping places on a wet night, and see half a dozen trolleybuses pass on without stopping; or he ought to be made to travel on a Chesterfield trolley bus when a 'rush' period is on. I feel sure he would not envy the lot of a sardine in a box.'

The letter went on to state that the single-deckers quickly filled up at busy periods and ignored subsequent stopping-places as there was simply no room for further passengers. 'They are the least efficient form of transport on the road', he complained, 'for the simple reason that they cannot and do not meet the demand made on them. Really they are too small for busy towns. Very nice in dry weather, when half the people walk, but when everybody wants to ride, they are a complete failure.' 'To compare Chesterfield's trolleybuses with Sheffield's tramcars', was his final sally, 'is almost as bad as comparing a perambulator with a motor-car.'

In November the Routes and Fares Sub-Committee recommended an adjustment to the railless fares between Whittington Moor and New Whittington, but the only alterations seem to have been a halfpenny reduction between the Hare and Hounds and Brierley Street, and the lessening of Workmens' prices of a halfpenny between town and Brierley Street, and a similar cut between town and the New Whittington terminus. For the very last time it was decided to operate no Christmas services. The moquette seats in the Strakers and omnibuses had evidently not proved a success, and in February 1931 the committee recommended their replacement by leather upholstery as and when required. Over the year REV miles had risen to 520,946, and 5,702,884 travellers had been conveyed over this one route, though the last figure includes those carried by the supporting motorbuses. Again all Strakers had mileages in the 30,000 bracket, indeed department statistics showed that each trolleybus ran an average 126 miles a day at a speed of 10.7mph. No.15, with 39,131 was the hardest worked, and No.12 with 33,781 travelled the least, due to the fact that it had spent almost a month off the road in June-July 1929. The overhead had cost £769 to keep in repair, the vehicles £2,352 and £1,628 had been expended on tyres. Apart from traffic revenue at £33,383, parcels had brought in £45 and adverts £220.

On Monday 24 March another German deputation visited Thornfield to look over the undertaking. There were twenty-three visitors, led by Dr H.C. Goosens from Aachen, and included among the party was Dr Hein, Minister of Transport, and officials and engineers from firms such as Siemens and Krupp. The group expressed a keen interest in the railless side of the facility and were conveyed by Hoggard and Crossley in Straker 12 on a joyride to New Whittington. The local paper noted their apparent astonishment at the climbing ability of the REV as it ascended Whittington Hill, and were interested in the reverser at the village terminus, as well as in 'the local inhabitants' as though the latter were some diverting species from the remote regions of Patagonia. As well as complimenting Hoggard on the smooth running of the trolleybuses, the Germans were impressed by the well-maintained road surfaces which they contrasted with their own granite or cobbled highways. After expressing profuse thanks and inviting their hosts to visit their own systems, the delegation commenced a northern tour to inspect other undertakings.

The Routes and Fares Sub-Committee met on 16 May, one of the items on their agenda being a report by Hoggard on proposed extensions of the trackless routes to Newbold and Hasland. The latter had been one of the proposals listed at a sub-committee meeting on 13 September 1927, but the former seems to have been a new idea. The meeting deferred the question for the time being, and this may have been the last time that the expansion of the electric transport facility was considered. Hoggard later pointed out the snags in developing the REV side of the system. The main out-of-town problems were the low railway bridges crossing certain roads which limited the service to single-deckers, and on three sides of the borough rival company operators were running alongside the Corporation, which made it an unprofitable option to bear the cost of poles and wires in the face of petrol bus competition. It was apparently decided at this time that all future development of the undertaking would be by the more flexible motorbus.

A contemporary newspaper report mentioned a 'special brake' which seems to have been the new rheostatic one fitted to the Strakers in 1930. There is a report that BTH modified one trolleybus with a retarder in that year as an experiment, and such was the success of the trial that all the vehicles were subsequently re-braked. In November the committee, for the first time since 1917, sanctioned Hoggard to arrange a skeleton service for Christmas Day. Six Strakers, Nos 1, 6, 7, 8, 10 and 14 were out on the 25th, running a total of 582 miles.

The end-of-year figures showed an escalating use of the trackless which covered 557,348 miles during the period. Motorbus miles also climbed, showing that the Strakers were overextended, and new vehicles were needed. Most of the single-deckers ran well over 40,000 miles, with REV 12 leading the field with 44,771. Only three of the fleet failed to reach this figure, including 9, which, out of service for much of June, completed only 20,196 miles, way behind her sisters. Repairs and renewals came in at £586 for the overhead, and £975 for tyres. Trackless repairs totalled £2,539; 5,677,842 passengers used the service, and revenues were £33,231, augmented by £182 on adverts and £42 on parcels.

After many complaints in the local press over the summer of 1931, aimed at the petrol buses as well as the trackless, Hoggard opted to beef up the REV fleet with two double-deckers. These could only ply the original line, as the 14ft 10in Station Road low bridge prevented their deployment to New Whittington. He was authorised to tender for the purchase of two new railless and six double-deck motorbuses. Hoggard reported that the trolleybuses were necessary as the route 'needed augmenting by Petrol 'Buses at peak loading times.' The newcomers would 'meet the heavy loading and displace as far as possible the use of petrol 'buses on railless routes.' The estimated cost of the two vehicles was £3,500, and the tender of Ransomes, Sims & Jefferies of Ipswich at £1,750 each was recommended for acceptance. Application was made to the MoT for a £3,500 loan to cover the costs, Hoggard later explaining that the borrowing period was to be set at five years to enable the debt to be written off at the same time as that on the Strakers.

The first of the Leyland trackless demonstrators ran under Chesterfield wires on Saturday 22 August. No information survives as to why this vehicle came to be in town, as the committee had already decided to accept the Ransomes tender, but the forty-eight-seat double-decker, which had already been extensively tested on the Nechells route in Birmingham, stayed for some two months and completed 5,461 miles on the system. This prototype model TBD1, completed in January 1931, was basically a TD1 petrol chassis with a GEC WT25 65hp motor, and a GEC FA3B controller fitted in place of the petrol engine. It retained the half-cab and dummy radiator, with maintenance access via the bonnet side. Registered as OV 1175, chassis 60342, and numbered 19, the bus boasted a Short Bros Body and was of standard Leyland lowbridge design. The rugged-looking two-decker was confined to the 'Track' during its stay, and several photographs recorded its service in town. It last ran on 18 October, after which it presumably returned home. It was later converted back into a petrol bus and was sold to Jersey in 1934. After preservation it has appeared at rallies both as a Halifax, and latterly a Jersey motorbus.

After the MoT had sanctioned a loan for the two Ransomes, one of the elegant, streamlined buses was shown at the Commercial Motor Exhibition in London in November, before entering service in Chesterfield the following month. Both the forty-eight-seat D2s, order number 2143/4, body numbers 1329/1330, were very much up-to-date in appearance, design and equipment. The only concession to the older styling was in the curved 'piano front' step just below the front upper deck windows. The bodies were constructed of timber covered with aluminium panels, with drop windows in the lower saloon and half-drop ones on the top deck. The seats were covered in green leather and were described as being 'particularly comfortable.' Interior floors were of Eldorado cork tiles, specially laid and polished. As with the Strakers, the colour scheme was green and white, with front and rear numbers. The Corporation coat-of-arms was sported on the lower side panel in front of each rear wheel, and both shields were surrounded by the legend 'CHESTERFIELD CORPORATION TRANSPORT.'

The 18ft side-by-side booms were mounted on a Ransomes patent sub-base rather than directly onto the roof. The construction formed a brace, relieving roof stresses caused by the operation of the booms and the strains when the trolleys de-wired. The robust steel-framed chassis incorporated a low-loading platform for easy passenger access. The brakes included a

Peters air-pressure system acting on both front and rear wheels, and a hand-operated one. The Ransomes-built motor provided for two separate winding systems, with the single armature having a commutator at each end to utilize series/parallel control. The motor casing was bolted to the underside of brackets attached to chassis side members, ensuring rigidity but allowing ready removal of the unit when necessary. The motor was rated at 80bhp, each separate winding being assessed at 40. The BTH controller was of the contactor type, with a foot-operated drum type master controller and a seperately mounted contactor panel containing the switches controlling the main circuits. In all there were eleven notches, including three running ones, full series giving approximate half speed, full parallel and the last one which increased speed by field diversion. There was also a hand-worked reversing drum interlocked with the main controller. The trolley bases were of the special low type manufactured by Brecknell, Willis and Co., with Bonsor trolleyheads.

At the November Transport meeting the committee expressed 'its gratitude to, and its appreciation of' Hoggard's services. His efficient management had reduced the department's running costs by one penny a mile. The two double-deckers, carrying registration numbers RB 4690 and RB 4691, first ran under Corporation wires in early December 1931. No.16 completed fifty miles on Wednesday 2nd, and No.17 travelled sixty-one miles the following Saturday. Official photographs were taken of the latter on trials during this week, on the Burlington Street curve and at Brampton terminus. The day was wet, and the first shot was taken at 2.30 p.m., logged by the Crooked Spire clock. Pre-service shots were also taken of Ransomes 16 in the depot yard.

Despite the welcome introduction of the two-deckers on the 'Track', petrol buses still ran up a fair mileage on the REV route, though the totals fell after the Ransomes commenced regular running. They were in time to endure the heavy fogs, which swathed the district in late January and early February. In fact so well did the fleet staff carry out their duties in the murky conditions that the committee were moved to commend all employees 'on the excellent services rendered by them on the nights of 30 January and the 3 February last, when Chesterfield and district was enveloped by dense fogs.' The end-of-year statistics showed that the electric fleet covered 574,926 miles during 1931-1932, carrying 5,744,730 passengers. Most of the Strakers had mileages exceeding 40,000, though problems with 9 and 11 restricted them to 18,430 and 23,002 respectively. The two Ransomes each had over 10,000 miles on the clock since their December debut. Repairs and maintenance included £621 on the wires, £494 on bodies and fittings, and £790 on tyres. Passenger revenue was £33,768, with £33 profit on parcels and £182 on advertising.

Free monthly timetables were provided for public use under Hoggard's *aegis*. The one for December 1932 is a neat little booklet of thirty-two pages, listing all the Corporation bus services, plus advertisements placed by local firms and businesses. On 7 December the Routes and Fares Sub-Committee discussed a report from Hoggard on the renewal of the overhead. He stated that 'the overhead line is worn out, and is causing serious anxiety regarding its safety.' He proposed replacement with 4/0 Abrasion Resisting Wire at an estimated cost of £1,973. Estler Bros of London submitted a tender at this price and the Town Clerk was authorised to apply to the MoT for a loan, repayable within five years.

The New Year of 1933 came in quietly, but heavy blizzards swept the district over the last weekend in February, making many roads impassable. The transport fleet however seems to have experienced little difficulty in fulfilling their obligations, and the daily mileages on the days of the snowstorms were little down on the norm, due presumably to efficient clearing. In March the MoT sanctioned a loan of £1,773 for the replacement of the trolley lines, the £200 reduction on the estimated costs being explained as credits available on the old wiring.

Work commenced on the removal of the worn running wire on Sunday 19 March when an abbreviated service was run entirely by petrol buses. The Brampton section was tackled first, and motorbuses operated on this route until Friday 7 April, while the trackless worked through to Whittington. On Sunday 26 March and 2 April the whole electric service was suspended in favour of petrol vehicles. The REVs were tested under Brampton wires on the afternoons of 25 and 31 March, and both sections were tried out on 1 April. Both routes closed down again on the 6 and 7 April, then through-running followed for two days before the commencement of the restringing of the Whittington line. The closure of this section lasted till the afternoon of 13 April, then it was reopened, only to close for another $2\frac{1}{2}$ days, from the 19th to the afternoon of the 21st. The final touches to the whole operation were carried out on the 25th, when all the trolleybuses were garaged, and the following day when the Brampton part of the system was closed to the railless for the last time. The trackless fleet reopened normal services on the 27 April, when the motorbuses were finally withdrawn.

The yearly figures showed that the trolleybuses had run 580,014 miles, ferrying 5,533,188 riders. Maintenance included £633 on the overhead, £2123 on the buses and £670 on tyres. Most of the REVs had mileages in the 37,000-40,000 bracket, led by No.10 with 40,905 miles, followed by double-decker 17 with 40,529. For the third year running 9 and 11 failed to pull their weight, the former managing a mere 13,632 miles, the latter 18,468, well below the contributions of their stablemates. A sign of the times was the decision to allow the Watch Committee to set up traffic lights on trolley poles at the junctions of Holywell Street and Park Road. These were doubtless connected with the increase in road traffic and the dangerous nature of these parts of the highway.

The late Len Rhodes and Bill Crampton worked for the department during the trackless era, the former in the garage, the latter as a conductor on the REVs. Len remembered some of the problems with the trolleybuses, particularly the Strakers with their long booms. The through-town route had a number of sharp bends, and the extra length of the trolleypoles created a 'whip' effect which could lead to the booms flying off the overhead. Len recalled taking a replacement REV up into town one day and rounding the Holywell Street-Stephenson Place curve at too wide an angle, whereupon the poles jumped off the wires and embedded themselves in the fancy leaded windows of the 'Picture House' Cinema. He duly received a roasting from the Deputy Manager, Crossley, but otherwise emerged unscathed. He also remembered how the whip effect of trolleyarms springing off the overhead could snap off trolleyheads, which could fly away and apparently vanish. One did a disappearing act between the Royal Hospital and the Grammar School, leaving the single-decker stranded. Careful searches failed to find the missing unit, which was later returned to the department from Wakefield, via the firm into whose open lorry it had fallen! Equally puzzling was the fate of another, which was lost on Holywell Cross, and was only retrieved when some sharp-eyed person noticed a hole in the roofing slates of a building lining the road. The trolleyhead duly turned up in the attic of the house.

Even more embarassing was the accident to the official car of the vehicle examiner for the Chesterfield district. On a visit to Thornfield he was foolish enough to park alongside one of the Strakers whose trolley housing was so weakened by rust that it broke away from the bus roof and deposited itself on top of his conveyance. His comments were not apparently recorded. Len also recalled how dangerous the Dark Lane corner was in foggy weather. It was apparently the custom in really thick fogs to station men with flares to guide trolleybuses round the tricky bend.

Bill Crampton had many reminiscences of his time as a conductor on the railless. One incident, hilarious in retrospect, also took place at Dark Lane one night when his driver noticed one of the Ransomes stationary at the roadside, having de-wired on the corner. Torches were necessary to locate the poles, and it took the crewmen of both vehicles to illuminate and pull down the heavy booms. The conductor of the Ransomes, Stan Littlewood, a small and wizened individual, was given the trolley ropes to hold, and great was the consternation a few minutes later when he could not be found. A strangled cry from above alerted his companions to the fact that Stan was suspended in mid-air, clinging on to the boom ropes for dear life! The trolley springs had proved too strong for his light weight, and he had been dragged upwards when left holding the ropes on his own.

One local butcher, who shall remain nameless, was so penny-conscious that if he arrived at the Brampton terminus a little beforehand, set off down Chatsworth Road in an effort to reach the Heaton Street fare stage and thus save a halfpenny! Bill's driver, usually Spencer White, would set off slightly early and they would invariably catch their prey by the St Thomas' Church stop, where they could exact the full 2d. Tommy Evans, the local photographer whose shop was on West Bars, was sometimes known to quit the trolleybus in a merry condition, and leave his camera and tripod behind, to be returned to him the following day.

A number of photographs show Strakers at the Brampton terminus parked behind a scale model of one of the REVs. This had been constructed by young Eric Chambers, who lived nearby, and who is usually seen posed by his creation. Eric was regarded as being only 'tenpence to the shilling' but he must have had some abilities to scratch-build the workmanlike replica shown in the photographs. Bill recalled that Eric was a real trolleybus enthusiast, and he often met the service cars by the loop. Occasionally he was given a free ride down Chatsworth Road as far as St Thomas' Church.

In September the Leyland Co. supplied a second trolleybus for extended trials on the Chesterfield system. The firm were then building a new range of trackless vehicles, designed as such, as distinct from modified petrol buses. The TSB1 was a single-deck prototype with a two-axle chassis and fitted with a front-mounted motor. The REV was neat in design, and probably had a central entrance. Twin headlights were recessed in the front dash, and the bus bore the logo 'LEYLAND TROLLEY BUS' on the panels just behind the driver's compartment on each side. Unfortunately the colour scheme is unknown, though photographs show it was plain, with no lining-out. It was thought that the single-decker ran unregistered, but the mileage book shows that it bore the number plate TJ 2822 while under the town's wires. The Leyland made its first appearance on 19 September, when it completed some 155 miles. From then onwards it was in regular service, operating most days throughout the autumn and early winter. TJ 2822 clocked up nearly 9,000 miles in Chesterfield, signing off on 11 December with 8,964.4 miles to its credit.

Sometime during this year the department began repainting the Strakers in a revised and more elaborate colour scheme. The new design included a frontal coat-of-arms surrounded by the words 'CHESTERFIELD CORPORATION TRANSPORT', replacing the number, which was now carried only on the rear of each bus. The side shields were moved forward of the centre entrance, and the front and back of each trolleybus, and the lower green body panels were elaborately lined-out in gold, giving each bus a smart and neat appearance. The Ransomes seem to have been redecorated after the single-deckers, as photographs taken in March 1934 show Strakers in the new livery, but Ransomes 16 in its original colours. No.17 was certainly repainted by November of that year, as a photograph taken after a collision with a lorry shows the revised paint job. It became easy to identify each two-decker as after their refurbishment 16 had a horizontal green band painted between the upper and lower saloons, while 17 retained its original white. Frontal shields replaced numbers on both Ransomes, though the flanking coats-of-arms were left in their former positions.

The 1933-1934 statistics showed that the trolleybuses had only marginally increased their mileages and passengers over the year. The REVs had run 588,536 miles, conveying 5,552,016 travellers, but none of the Strakers had covered 40,000 miles, the leader being No.1 with 38,961, though both the Ransomes had exceeded this figure. Again Strakers 9 and 11 lagged behind their companions, with 26,538 and 25,326 miles respectively. Repairs and maintenance included £242 spent on the overhead, £2,041 on chassis and bodies, plus £438 on tyres. Traffic revenue was £32,661, with £26 gleaned from parcels and £149 on adverts. Trolleybus traction seemed set for an extended stay in the town, with Hoggard praising it as 'efficient, reliable, safe and to inspire confidence in a densely populated area.'

Little of note transpired over the year, the electric service apparently functioning smoothly and efficiently over the summer and autumn. On 13 November however Ransomes 17 suffered an accident which kept it off the road for over a month. It was a morning of dense fog and on Sheffield Road, near the junction with Hazelhurst Lane, the double-decker, driven by William

Boam, was involved in a front offside collision with a lorry driven by Wilfred Clough from Leeds. The REV suffered severe localised damage, as did the lorry, while both drivers were slightly injured. No.17 was not back in service until 15 December, and claims for personal and other harm were not settled until February 1936.

There were two occasions in December and January when the power supply failed, once for twenty minutes on 20 December, and again for an unspecified time on 24 January. On the latter date petrol buses had to replace the trackless, running seventy-one miles before the current was restored. These occasions increased considerably during the last three years of trolleybus operation. At a meeting on 14 February, the Routes and Fares Sub-Committee approved the amendment of fares on the Chesterfield-New Whittington railless route. The fares schedule was published on 7 March, and the revised prices are shown on the illustrated poster.

End-of-year figures showed a rise in the 1934-1935 mileage to 606,806, ferrying 5,640,405 passengers, another increase over the previous twelve months. Most single-deckers recorded mileages in the 35,000-39,000 bracket, REV 2 leading the field with 39,885. Those two lame ducks, 9 and 11, still lagged behind the rest with 26,538 and 25,326 miles respectively. Both double-deckers broke the 40,000 barrier with No.16 recording 44,233 miles over the year. £342 had been expended on the wiring, £2,486 on bodies and chassis, and £568 on tyres. Revenue was £33,075, with parcels raising £32 and adverts £53.

On two occasions during the summer of 1935 the power failed, once on 8 August when the overhead line broke, and on 8 September when the guard wire near the Grammar School snapped and fell across the power lines, cutting off the current. Repairs were quickly effected, and the service was restored within twenty minutes. That same month the committee decided to lay the power cable at Whittington Hill underground, at an estimated coat of £75.

Hoggard was still seeking to augment the trolleybus fleet, and made enquiries about three Karrier Clough E4 single-deckers made redundant when York abandoned its single railless route in January 1935. The vehicles had been transferred to West Yorkshire Services in May and at the Transport Committee meeting on 19 November Hoggard was authorised to purchase the trio 'subject to their condition proving satisfactory on examination.' The elegant thirty-two-seat rear-entrance Roe-bodied REVs, built in 1931, were very much state-of-the-art when supplied. The bodies were low-loaders with two compartments, the rear for smokers, bottom frameworks of oak, and other frames and pillars of ash. The body panels were steel, with two Rawlings drop-windows on either side. All seating was transverse, and of semi-bucket style trimmed with cowhide, with grab handles on all gangway seats. Destination boxes were fitted front and rear, and the trolley bases were supported and fixed on pitch pine planks.

The interior lighting was by lamps fixed in the bulkheads, and easy riding was provided by long flat semi-elliptical springs on both front and rear axles. Foot and handbrakes were fitted, the former of internal expansion type, described as 'extremely smooth and powerful in action.' The wheelbase was 14ft 6in, and the turning circle 53ft. The single lightweight 65hp 110E BTH electric motor was mounted below the saloon floor. The contactor control equipment comprised a foot-operated accelerating master controller, a number of contactors mounted on panels, and a manually operated reverser. Foot operation left the driver's hands free for steering and applying the handbrake.

The trolleybase was designed to allow the Karrier to swing out from the running wire for a distance of 13ft in either direction at full speed, and the base embodied double sets of roller bearings for easy swivelling. The steel tube booms were 18ft long, with an upward set to maintain pressure on the lines. The chassis numbers were 55001-3, and the body numbers GO1873-5. While at York they were designated 30-32, and in their original livery possessed a spruce and up-to-date appearance. Hoggard's inspection was evidently satisfactory and they were purchased for £707, the cost to be defrayed from revenue. Their acquisition was announced at the 17 December gathering, though they must by then have arrived and were presumably redecorated in Chesterfield colours before commencing operations in early December. VY 2291 was numbered 18, VY 2292 19 and VY 2293 20. No.18 ran a short sixteen miles on the 6th, and all three were shown to the public a day later.

There was however another demonstration railless operating on the system from late November which stole some of the thunder from the second-hand Karriers. This splendid trolleybus was another Leyland prototype, described by the press as a 'new, super-luxury double-decked trackless trolleybus' and by a later writer as 'a unique and fascinating model.' It was designated TB10 and was a revolutionary design, a six-wheeler with two 40hp GEC traction motors, one mounted outside each chassis side frame. The 13ft 6in high 30ft long bus had electrically-operated front and rear doors fitted into a Massey lowheight body, seating thirty-four passengers upstairs and twenty-nine down. Riders entered by the rear doors and exited via the front. Completed in early 1935, this magnificent conveyance was fitted with air brakes as standard, and its turning arc was a creditable 58ft. The colour scheme has not been recorded, but a white band below the lower-deck windows bore on both sides the legend 'LEYLAND LOW-LOADING TROLLEY BUS.'

The TB10, which came directly to town from the Commercial Motor Show, first operated in Chesterfield on 29 November, when its sleek modern appearance and high degree of comfort probably created a minor sensation. Its registration plate is usually given as TJ 9010, though photographs show that a temporary number, 052 TB was also carried. However the mileage book shows that while in Chesterfield this splendid two-decker operated as ATD 747. The big Leyland ran for sixteen days between the end of November and 1 January 1936, completing 1,278 miles and giving the local ratepayers a taste of real luxury travel. The bus was demonstrated to a number of operators, but remains unique and incredibly its fate is unknown. Regrettably no photographs of its Chesterfield sojourn appear to have survived, if any were ever taken.

The three Karriers were speedily integrated into the trolleybus system and by the beginning of 1936 were in regular running order. Railless mileage continued to rise, to 629,387 in 1935-1936, doubtless due to the new vehicles. Travellers too rose to 5,879,421. Trackless revenue was £34,005 with parcels realising £37 and advertising £48. Overhead maintenance was £359, bodies and chassis £2,023 and tyres £593. The Strakers all recorded very similar mileages, between 34,000-38,000. No.6 travelled the furthest, 38,822 miles, and even the underused 9 and 11 pulled their weight with over 37,000 and 36,000 miles respectively. Both Ransomes again ran over 41,000 miles each, while the new Karriers averaged over 8,000 apiece. The purchase of the ex-York single-deckers suggested that the Corporation had no intention of abandoning electric traction, which seemed set to stay.

July saw the commencement of an annoying series of power failures which lasted well into 1937. On the 17th the Whittington current failed, while on 1 August, a busy Saturday night, the New Whittington supply was cut off from 10.07 p.m. to 11.25 p.m. There were further current breaks on 27 August, 4 September, 31 October (a half-hour stoppage), and 7 November. This spate of current loss was followed by a series of impenetrable fogs which blanketed the town and its environs over the weekend of 20-22 November. The local paper noted that 'one of the worst fogs for many years enveloped the district.' On Sunday the 22nd the trolleybuses, which usually averaged 950 miles on that day, only completed 260, the shortfall being made up by motorbuses. When the fog eventually cleared electric power was again cut, as the running wire was pulled down on the 23rd, and was not fully repaired for three days. Petrol buses had to take over REV duties along part of the system, and over the six days they totted up nearly 1,000 miles on the route. Fog again bedevilled the trackless service on 9 December. This must have been another severe visitation, as the Transport Committee, at its meeting on the 15th, requested Hoggard to 'convey to the employees in the Department the congratulations of the Committee upon the manner in which the transport services were conducted during the recent fog.'

The fogs again swirled in during mid-January 1937, and were once more followed by current failures on the 18th, and on 6 and 9 February, again requiring motorbus substitution. Len Rhodes remembered that while the power to the lines was working two lights on a panel at

Thornfield remained constantly illuminated. When the current failed the lights went out and it was all hands to the pumps to get standby vehicles out on the road to rescue stranded passengers. After this series of mishaps to the overhead supply, conditions returned to normal and no more failures were reported during the year or so still left to the trolleybuses.

The last full year of trackless operation showed another slight rise in mileage and passengers. The former totalled 638,363 and the latter climbed above six million for the first time, to 6,006,998. Line maintenance was £169, bodies and chassis £1,997 and tyres £590. Revenue worked out at £35,131 with £39 for parcels and £72 for advertising. With the arrival of the Karriers, Straker mileage declined, and all but one vehicle averaged 32,000-36,000 miles each. Straker 6 again led the field with 36,191 miles, while the odd-man-out was again the inevitable 9, which ran 31,311 miles. Again the Ransomes were worked hard, with 16 and 17 exceeding 44,000, while the Karriers completed between 22,000 and 25,000 miles each.

A number of views exist of Eric Chambers and the model of the Straker he built himself. Here he poses at Brampton terminus by REV 2, whose ugly advertising boards remain for the moment unsullied. The driver is John McDonald, and the diminutive conductor second from right is Bill Crampton, whose reminisences appear in the text. (*A.R. Kaye*)

Eric again, this time in front of Straker 7 driven by W.E. Smith, in front of an appreciative crowd. Note that the speed limit for the trackless has now risen to 16mph. (*A.R. Kaye*)

On 23 March 1930 the Transport Committee used Straker 12 for a municipal joyride when they entertained a German deputation touring English transport systems. Here the group enbus at Thornfield for a trip to New Whittington. Transport Manager Richard Hoggard, in his favourite bowler, can be seen on the right. (*Chesterfield Borough*)

## Chesterfield Corporation Transport Department.

# RAILLESS FARES AND STAGES.

**ORDINARY FARES.** | **WORKMEN'S FARES.**

### BRAMPTON SECTION.

| | Fare Stage No. | Barker Lane | Heaton Street | Brampton |
|---|---|---|---|---|
| | | d. | d. | d. |
| Chesterfield (Stephenson Place) ... | 1 | 1 | 1½ | 2 |
| Faijambe Road ... | 2 | 1 | 1½ | |
| Barker Lane ... | 3 | 1 | | |
| Heaton Street ... | 4 | 1 | | |
| Brampton Terminus ... | 5 | — | | |

### BRAMPTON SECTION. (Workmen's)

| | |
|---|---|
| Chesterfield and Heaton Street | 1d. |
| Faijambe Road and Brampton Terminus | 1d. |
| Chesterfield and Brampton Terminus | 1½d. |

### WHITTINGTON SECTION.

| | Fare Stage No. | Hare and Hounds | Nelson Street | Whittington Moor | Cock and Magpie | Brierley Street | New Whittington |
|---|---|---|---|---|---|---|---|
| | | d. | d. | d. | d. | d. | d. |
| Chesterfield Market Place ... | 1 | 1 | 1½ | 2 | 3 | 3½ | 4 |
| Albert Street ... | 2 | | 1 | 1½ | 2½ | 3 | 3½ |
| Hare and Hounds and Nelson St. ... | 3 & 4 | | | 1 | 2 | 2½ | 3 |
| Whittington Moor ... | 5 | | | | 1 | 1½ | 2 |
| Cock and Magpie ... | 6 | | | | | 1 | 1½ |
| Brierley Street ... | 7 | | | | | | 1 |
| New Whittington ... | 8 | | | | | | — |

### WHITTINGTON SECTION. (Workmen's)

| | Fare Stage No. | Nelson Street | Whittington Moor | Cock and Magpie | Brierley Street | New Whittington |
|---|---|---|---|---|---|---|
| | | d. | d. | d. | d. | d. |
| Chesterfield ... | 1 | 1 | 1½ | 2½ | 2½ | 3 |
| Albert Street ... | 2 | | 1 | 2 | 2 | 2½ |
| Hare and Hounds and Nelson St. ... | 3 | | 1 | 1½ | 2 | 2½ |
| Whittington Moor ... | 4 | | | 1 | 1½ | |
| Cock and Magpie ... | 5 | | | | 1 | |
| New Whittington ... | 6 | | | | — | |

WORKMEN'S FARES OPERATE TO 9 A.M. FROM EACH TERMINUS.

TRANSPORT OFFICES,
THORNFIELD, CHESTERFIELD,
(Telephone 3357 and 3053).
30th October, 1930.

R. HOGGARD, M. Inst. T.,
GENERAL MANAGER.

In October 1930 trolleybus fares were reduced across the board. The plate shows the revised schedule approved by the manager on the 30th of the month.

A fairly unrecognisable part of the trackless route, Canal Wharf, at the bottom of Hardwick Street, was where depot-bound Strakers entered Thornfield from the rear. A trolleybus is parked in the garage yard, in front of the crews' recreation room. (*Chesterfield Borough*)

Canal Wharf formed part of a road-widening scheme, put into operation in the early 1930s. The plate shows clearly the rear entrance for the trolleybuses, with one car in the yard, and the rear of another just visible between the sliding doors. (*Chesterfield Borough*)

Straker 9, rather a lame duck in its early years, heads past the Market Hall on its way to Brampton some time in the early 1930s. Note the white-coated policeman directing operations behind the bus. *(A.R. Kaye)*

An excellent shot of the 'hangar' doors and exit wiring for the REVs emerging from the Thornfield Garage. Straker 9 poses alongside a Bristol motorbus, completely dwarfing its stablemate. *(Chesterfield Transport)*

REV 9 again, photographed at the same time as the previous plate. Note the terms offered by the Furniture Exchange Company, and the repositioning of the Corporation coat-of-arms, perhaps part of an experimental livery heralding a revised design scheme. (*Local Studies Library*)

An interesting 'trolleyscape' showing a fairly narrow Corporation Street in 1931, with two trolleybuses visible in the distance, one heading towards Whittington, the other to Stephenson Place.

Compare this vista with the last, taken in late 1936 after road widening, demolition and the building of the prestigious shops and 'Regal' cinema on the left. The cinema opened for business in October of that year with the Astaire/Rogers hit *Follow the Fleet*, which also starred Randolph Scott! (*A.R. Kaye*)

A rare bird was this prototype Leyland lowbridge double-deck TBD1 trolleybus demonstrator (OV 1175), seen here at the Market Place Railway Station. The conveyance arrived on 22 August 1931 and stayed in town for just under two months. Excursions available from the station included Cruden Bay and the Forth Bridge, Scotland. (*H.J. Morgan*)

At the Brampton terminus the long-boomed Leyland tests itself on the loop. Note the rugged and uncompromising lines of the half-cab Lancastrian, which was basically a converted petrol bus. (*A.R. Kaye*)

The big Leyland pauses outside Hadfield's shop on High Street, attracting some interest from passers-by. However, rival transport, stoically plodding past, registers supreme indifference towards the newcomer. (*A.R. Kaye*)

An elegant arrival was this Ransomes D2, one of two ordered by Hoggard to supplement the electric fleet. These very much state-of-the-art vehicles arrived in November 1931. Here No.16 (RB 4890) poses, trolleys down, soon after arrival at Thornfield. The double-deckers could not deploy beyond Whittington Moor due to the low bridge at Sheepbridge. (*H.J. Morgan*)

Ransomes 16 shows off its advanced lines at the depot, revealing details of its low-loading rear exit. This streamlined conveyance could carry forty-eight passengers, sixteen more than the single-deck Strakers. (*Chesterfield Transport*)

At Brampton, Ransomes 17 tries its 19ft booms on the turning loop, here seen to advantage. This is one of the few views known showing the nearside of these double-deckers, and picks out their salient features. (*H.J. Morgan*)

A fine study of Ransomes 17 (RB 4981) under Chesterfield wires at the Burlington Street corner on 5 December1931, three days after its stablemate's debut. The time on this wet, winter day is accurately logged by the Crooked Spire clock. *(H.J. Morgan)*

Leyland tested out their single-deck TSB1 over a three-month period in Chesterfield in late 1933. Here the smart-looking REV is pictured operating under South Lancs. wires just before its arrival in town. *(Chesterfield Transport)*

The TBS1 ran in Chesterfield with the registration TJ 2822. Though it completed some 9,000 miles on the railless route, the only shot of the vehicle to surface is this slightly blurred effort taken on Sheffield Road near Pottery Lane on the way to town. (C.C. Hall)

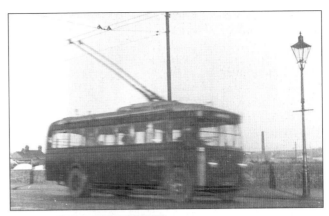

*Middle:* Straker 15 in the revised livery introduced *c.*1933 pauses on the Stephenson Place turn under the one-way wiring via Holywell Street. The view can be closely dated by that week's offering at the 'Picture House' Cinema on the right, reflected in the bus's side windows, a British farce called *Up to the Neck*. This masterpiece was showing in late March 1934. (G.H.F. *Atkins*)

*Bottom:* Straker 12 waits in its new livery opposite the Terminus Hotel – sadly demolished by the council in July 2002 – another Atkins study of March 1934, taken on a visit to the town. Note the section box behind the conductor and the good view of the frontal shield now sported by the single-deckers. (G.H.F. *Atkins*)

**CHESTERFIELD CORPORATION TRANSPORT DEPT.**

# NEW WHITTINGTON SECTION

## Commencing Monday, 1st April, 1935

New Stage Fares as set out below will come into operation :—

| | |
|---|---|
| CHESTERFIELD and NEW WHITTINGTON | 3½d. |
| CHESTERFIELD and "COCK & MAGPIE," OLD WHITTINGTON | 2½d. |
| CHESTERFIELD and BRIERLEY STREET | 3d. |
| ALBERT STREET and "COCK & MAGPIE" | 2d. |
| " " " BRIERLEY STREET | 2½d. |
| " " " NEW WHITTINGTON | 3d. |
| "HARE & HOUNDS" and "COCK & MAGPIE" | 1½d. |
| " " " " BRIERLEY STREET | 2d. |
| " " " " NEW WHITTINGTON | 2½d. |
| WHITTINGTON MOOR and "COCK & MAGPIE" | 1d. |
| " " " BRIERLEY STREET | 1½d. |
| " " " NEW WHITTINGTON | 2d. |
| "COCK & MAGPIE" and NEW WHITTINGTON | 1d. |

CHILDREN'S FARES:

Children up to 5 years of age Free, and between 5 and 14, half the adult fare, with a minimum fare of 1d.

R. HOGGARD, M.Inst.T.,
General Manager,
7th March, 1935.

Thornfield Depot,
Sheffield Road,
Chesterfield.     Tel. 2357.

*Left:* In March 1935 fares on the New Whittington section were scheduled for reduction across the board. The leaflet illustrated shows the new stage prices, which commenced on 1 April.

A weathered-looking Ransomes 16, still in its original paintwork, caught by Atkins on the West Bars loop by Nadin's shop. By this time the Strakers had been decorated in a new style. (*G.H.F. Atkins*)

In 1934 traffic lights appeared at Holywell Cross, and Eyre's premises occupied the opposite corner. The left-hand running wire took town-bound buses on the Stephenson Place one-way system, while Whittington REVs used the opposite overhead. The date is November 1935, established by the sign on the right, advertising *Gold-Diggers of 1935* with Dick Powell and Gloria Stuart, showing at the 'Picture House' Cinema that month. (*Chesterfield Borough*)

Cavendish Street corner in transition that same month with Knifesmithgate showing off its fine new mock-Tudor buildings. Note the single line of running wire going left to right, joined by the turning loop for trolleybuses on the short-running to Whittington. (*Chesterfield Borough*)

Another excellent 'trolleyscape' at the junction of Sheffield and Newbold Roads, with the overhead carried on twin poles and span wire, with numerous supporting 'pull-offs.' A smart Rover saloon is parked on the left, and the trolley standards have acquired litter bins. (*Chesterfield Borough*)

York Karrier E4 No.32 in pristine condition in front of the Fulford Road Depot in 1932. York's mini trolleybus system was abandoned in 1935 and the three railless cars were purchased by Hoggard for the bargain-basement price of £707. They commenced running in town in early December 1935. (*Chesterfield Transport*)

This superb TB10 double-deck Leyland was the last prototype demonstrator to run under the town's wires, and gave Cestrefeldians the chance to sample some real luxury travel. Operating with the registration ATD 747, this advanced vehicle covered 1,278 miles between November 1935 and January 1936. (*Chesterfield Transport*)

Some scenes taken late in the local trackless era include this study of Straker 7 picking up trade outside the High Street post office with some solidly-built motor cars in shot.

Straker 1 parks at the Brampton loop at 12.42 p.m. according to the bus shelter clock. This side view gives a good illustration of the later colour scheme adopted by these conveyances. Cleveland petrol, at 1s 4d per gallon, is now just a fond memory! (*Local Studies Library*)

An interesting vista of Stephenson Place *c*.1931, displaying well the overhead lines, including the loop for vehicles turning right past the bank façade into Cavendish Street on the left. The mock-Tudor fronted 'Picture House' Cinema appears in the distance, to the left of the Bristol motorbus waiting at the Staveley stop.

Contrast this *c*.1937 shot with the above. Straker 8 awaits trade at the Brampton stop, whilst a Titan TD3 double-decker has replaced the Bristol. The taxi opposite the REV has apparently not moved since the previous view was taken! Note how the camera has totally failed to pick up the overhead wiring. (*A.R. Kaye*)

Along Burlington Street, No.11 poses for its picture in the narrow confines of this thoroughfare, against the imposing backdrop of the Parish Church. No one seems to be rushing to avail themselves of Burton's Tailors offer of 'A 5 Guinea Suit for 45/-.' The shop is still there, but not, alas, the same bargains!

In 1937 Charles Hall took a number of views of the system, including this shot of an unidentified Straker easing its 26ft length round the Black Horse loop on its way to New Whittington. The inn has since been demolished. (*C.C. Hall*)

Two Strakers work the route on either side of the Whittington turning circle, the left-hand one on its way back to Chesterfield, the nearest pausing by the Black Horse loop, on Station Road, picking up passengers for New Whittington. The long-defunct 'Lyceum' Cinema stands on the left. (*C.C. Hall*)

By luck Hall travelled on a Karrier to New Whittington, taking several shots of the photographically under-represented ex-York trolleybuses. Here Karrier 19 heads along High Street, with Stone Lane on the right. (*C.C. Hall*)

The Karrier moves towards the reverser, giving a good view of its rear entrance, while the conductor carefully oversees the operation. The taller block of houses on the right still remain. (*C.C. Hall*)

Karrier 19 backs into Stone Lane, with the conductor keeping a watchful eye on the trolleybooms as they engage the automatic frogs which positioned them on the return wires. The elegant lines of the REV show up well in this view. (*C.C. Hall*)

In Stephenson Place Karrier 20 waits at the Brampton bus stop, opposite Deacon's Bank. Unlike No.19 this vehicle mounts an extra fog or spot lamp. (*C.C. Hall*)

A somewhat blurred view, but worth including as shots of the Ransomes are uncommon. Here No.17 climbs Stonegravels Hill on the way to town, opposite the entrance to Stonegravels Lane. The large gabled house behind the trolleybus, once the offices of the Cleansing Department, has since been demolished. (*C.C. Hall*)

Straker 12 remains an innocent bystander in this accident at the junction of Chatsworth and Walton Roads, near Pearson's Pottery, on 10 August 1937. The main protagonists were the Shentall's van and the Wolseley on the left. One of the Ransomes can just be picked out in the distance, and the span wiring shows up well. A police sergeant keeps a watching brief on events. (*Local Studies Library*)

# Nine

# Railless Replacement
# 1937-1938

Although rumours had been in the air for some time it must have surprised many who read the Transport Committee proceedings of 11 May to note that Hoggard had prepared a document considering 'the future policy to be adopted in respect of the Brampton to New Whittington trolley omnibus service.' The Town Clerk and Transport Manager were authorised to meet the Traffic Commissioners, who regulated all bus services under the 1930 Road Traffic Act, on the matter, and report to the next committee meeting. Hoggard later recalled the reasons for a proposed changeover, and the 'flutter' it had caused when the news was first announced. Many transport authorities had contacted him for details, questioning how a corporation running its own electricity undertaking would sanction such a step. There were also queries from the Coal Utilisation Board, the manufacturers of electrical equipment, and the Mining Association. The news of the recommendation to scrap the trolleybuses had leaked out in certain circles, and the pros and cons had been keenly debated behind the scenes.

The general public had a chance to experience motorbus travel over the trolley route in June, when a road-widening scheme along Cavendish Street resulted in a close-down of the whole line from Tuesday the 15th to Friday the 18th inclusive, followed by five days from the 21st to the 25th. The previous Monday the 14th saw a restricted REV service. Trolleybuses 1, 3, 8, 9, 12 and 16 ran some 798 miles on that day. For much of the following fortnight it was felt necessary to shut off the current, though a shortened service could have been operated from the depot to New Whittington and back. The department chose however to keep the trackless in the garage and operate petrol buses over the nine days they needed to complete the road operations. The REVs were back on the road for Saturday 25 June.

At the committee gathering on 21 June Hoggard and the Borough Treasurer reported on the financial aspects of the policy of trolleybus abandonment, and then Hoggard and the Town Clerk discussed their meeting with the Traffic Commissioners. The upshot was that the Town Council were recommended to substitute motorbuses for REVs on the trackless route as and from 1 April 1938. The *Times*, in its issue of 2 July, expressed its opinions on the proposed change. 'When one considers the fierce controversy that raged ten years ago over the installation of the trolleybuses in preference to motor-buses', ran the editorial, 'one is inclined to rub one's eyes, but it must be admitted that there are many new factors in the situation today.' On Tuesday 6 July the full council, with forty members present, moved to propose the approval of the minutes of the Transport Committee, recommending the abandonment of railless traction. There was an amendment to refer the minute on future policy back, but this was defeated with only six dissentients.

Philip Robinson, once so staunch a promoter of the trolleybuses, estimated that new diesel buses would provide a profit of £10,536 over the next six years as against £6,381 for the REVs. He felt there would be just as great a local demand for coal whether the trolley fleet ran or not. The system had just cleared a ten-year debt of £72,343, including an existing tramway debt of £23,415, a road renewal debt of £11,876 and £37,052 for the original trackless fleet. The trolleybuses had started in 1937 completely free of debt, and Robinson was confident that what they had done with the REVs they could easily do with diesel transport. Councillor Oliver Wright was the most forthright opponent of the new scheme, feeling that it meant scrapping home fuel sources and substituting foreign oil. He was unconvinced that oil was cheaper, and if war broke out there was more security in electricity; indeed, most towns and cities were developing their electrical services. Robinson was sympathetic to Wright's concerns, but as far as international troubles were concerned, he had no doubt that 'if this country is mad enough to go to war, or to be dragged into war, the only transport you will be interested in will be either a hearse or a yellow cab.' One wonders if he recalled his words two years later, when the trolley fleet was long gone and war clouds darkened the horizon.

The *Sheffield Independent* in its 8 July issue, praised Wright's 'tactful and reasonable' opposition to the trackless proposal. He was reported as not using 'any of the tricks of oratory, nor did he attempt to hammer his opinions into his colleagues; he pointed out in quiet but impressive manner that he was not convinced of the advantage of diesel oil over electricity locally, that he believed there was a risk involved in the change; and he advocated a waiting period in which the Council could search for further information before surrendering their rights.' Other councillors were sure the decision was right, offering the chance to dismantle the 'glorified birdcage' and remove 'the murky cobwebs stretched across a darkened sky.' The ubiquitous Councillor Rogers was there to condemn the trackless as 'the slowest form of transport that could be possibly found in the county. A boy on a bicycle would always beat a trolleybus from New Whittington to Whittington Moor,' though Wright stressed the environmental assets of the enterprise, claiming that 'at least the electrical service was a clean service, and they did not get the smell.'

In a later speech to the East Midlands Section of the Institute of Transport at Nottingham, Hoggard outlined the reasons why he advised abandonment of a transport system that had been an undoubted success during its working life. He mentioned the snags that prevented the extension of electric traction in the locality, including the GPO telephone trunk lines strung at low height along the trackless route, which prevented span-wire deployment and necessitating the use of long bracket arms, the lengthiest allowed by the MoT. The GPO would only bury these lines if the Corporation was willing to foot the bill. He was not impressed when the GPO asked the department to fit coils or compressors to the REVs to stop wireless interference at the latter's expense! Needless to say this was never done, and radio enthusiasts along the line had to put up with impaired reception every time a railless whined by.

At four points along the route the electric fleet had to pull towards the road centre to avoid de-wirement, a risky procedure with no chance of amendment until the seventy or so trunk telephone lines were removed. Practically all the possible out-of-town trolleybus extensions were bedevilled by low railway bridges crossing main roads, though single-deckers could have operated along them. However, along other viable routes the Corporation ran in competition with other companies, making it unprofitable to set up poles and overhead. Hence motor omnibuses were used to develop these localities.

The Manager also pointed out that when they purchased the two Ransomes in 1931 they were busy considering future department policy, and consequently wrote off the new trolleybus debt in five years, the same time that the Straker debt was due for settlement. Thus by 1937 the electric bus facility was free of its costs, having paid off all charges. If trolleybuses were to be retained a good deal of money needed to be spent on the enterprise. New overhead wiring was necessary, plus a new sub-station to meet the increased load, and new trolley standards to replace those of 1904 vintage. Hoggard also considered that current, at .740d per unit was at least .240d too high. An electrical engineer had recently told him that any electricity department that could not supply .6d for the day load, and .4d for the night, needed both the engineer and his department 'attending to.' One hopes the Chesterfield engineer was not too put out by these apparent criticisms!

Hoggard and his committee felt the diesel bus could do all that the REV could do; it could carry as big a load, and negotiate roads just as well. It could overtake more safely without risk of de-wirement, and had powers of acceleration equal to or better than the trackless. Unsightly posts and wiring could be dispensed with, and the flexibility of the motorbus would enable the undertaking to vary services and introduce through-running between trackless routes and interlinking ones, hitherto impossible with the two classes of vehicle. Running costs being cheaper with diesels than REVs, there was no hesitation by Hoggard in recommending the way ahead.

After the great trolleybus battles of the mid-1920s, and Hoggard's earlier support for electric traction, he had come to the opinion that in Chesterfield's case the two classes of transport were having a deleterious effect on progress and efficiency. There was also the valid point that the department's drivers were expected to drive both types of bus, which must have been dangerous from a safety point of view. He felt that the trolleybuses had 'done admirably' but the flexibility offered by the new diesels convinced him that the town was ahead of the times, and that other authorities (including London Transport) were now doing what Chesterfield had done ten years ago in adopting the railless system. To Hoggard, the provinces always gave the lead to the capital, and he felt London would sooner or later convert to diesel buses at the expense of the trackless.

He also felt he had an answer to those who warned of fuel problems caused by any future war. His comments are poignant when one considers how times have changed since he made his speech. 'Even though diesel oil is brought from abroad', he noted, 'it comes in British tankers, it is handled by British ports, it is delivered to us in British-controlled lorries, with British labour, and how much is left for the foreigner after that?' He concluded that if hostilities did commence 'I should not give much for either the trolley bus or the diesel bus undertaking, and therefore the home-produced fuel argument carries little weight with me.'

Hoggard also praised his committee for backing his judgement, convinced he was recommending a transport network that was in the best interests of the town where he obtained his livelihood. There was little more to say; the die was cast and the trolley fleet was doomed to expire in less than a year. It is interesting to note that during the final few months of working, both the Ransomes and the Karriers, though newer than the Strakers, ran reduced mileages, with the original single-deckers carrying the main traffic burden. For many weeks from September onwards the Karriers ran very irregular schedules, with 18 only turning out on Saturdays, and 19 only appearing on odd occasions during the week. Fogs again swathed the district on 24 November and 19 December, but the trolleybuses coped with the poor weather efficiently enough.

The last year of trolleybus operation in Chesterfield began with the authorisation to sell off all the overhead equipment and the REVs. All electric cabling was also to be dispensed with in due course. The schedule of materials for disposal was listed in a letter of 16 February, and included over 16 tons of 4/0 wire and seven of 0/3 wire. A tender was requested for the removal of 538 traction poles, some with bracket arms, and the reinstatement of the roads. Some sixty standards holding electric or gas brackets were left in position until the street lighting was updated. Seven section boxes were also up for disposal, but the only trolley vehicles for sale were the Strakers, minus tyres. A Karrier K4 tower waggon with solid tyres, and a Heathman's tower were also thrown in, together with a host of spares for both the REVs and overhead. All tenders were to be delivered by 12 March 1938.

One wonders why the Strakers, only eleven years old and with plenty of future service in them, were not offered to any undertaking in need of augmenting its own electric fleet. It is even harder to perceive why the other vehicles, each less than seven years old, were not advertised to other authorities, who would surely have received bargains in purchasing these buses? As it was, all the equipment and the fourteen Strakers were sold to Devey Bros of Birmingham, scrap iron, steel and metal merchants, for a tender of £1,125 offered on 11 March. The sale price was accepted by the Transport Committee on 22 March.

As closedown approached, the double-deckers were withdrawn from weekday service and from 12 February onwards only operated on Saturdays, apart from a twenty-nine mile foray by No.17 on Monday 28 February. The Ransomes ran for the last time on Saturday 19 March. The other REVs maintained a heavy mileage during the last few weeks, averaging some 18,000-23,000 miles daily, except on Sundays when the average was around 1,100. Karrier 19 ran its last journeys on the 18th, though 19 went on to the 23rd, and 20, along with Straker 8, was selected for the ultimate run on the 24th. It had been decided to operate the railless-diesel changeover on Friday 25 March as this was the first day of the second licensing quarter. Consequently the trolleybuses were to be phased out on the evening of Thursday 24 March.

There is some debate as to the identity of the last service car to run on the evening of 24 March 1938. Straker 4 has been put forward for the honour, and the Report Sheet reproduced here lists the schedule, though it does appear that an unidentified REV followed the former, leaving town for Brampton at 7.35 p.m. No.4 left Stephenson Place at 6.54 p.m.

# Ten

# End of an Era
# 24 March 1938

The last day's railless service was a somewhat attenuated one, with only 550 miles recorded, as against 1,938 the previous Thursday. Presumably motorbuses augmented the trolleybuses on this day. Seven service vehicles were out, comprising 2, 4, 5, 7, 12, 14 and 15, all original Strakers. They clocked up 257 miles on the Brampton run, plus 293 to Whittington. There is some divergence as to the last operational bus, Straker 4 being claimed for the honour. It certainly ran the biggest mileage on the day, $134\frac{1}{2}$, comprising $17\frac{1}{2}$ journeys, $8\frac{1}{2}$ with driver Jack Dudson, including service on the 'Track' and two trips to New Whittington, $3\frac{3}{4}$ on the 'Track' with Fred Thompson and $5\frac{1}{4}$ including one journey to New Whittington with Laurie Gilsthorpe. He and his conductor, Harry Clarke, crewed REV 4's final run, claiming to have issued the last ticket on the system, a green 2d numbered HV 9397.

There is however some ambiguity about this claim, as the commencement of the last through trip was given as 6.54 p.m., while Hoggard, writing to Robinson on the 29 March, included a set of sixteen tickets issued on the 7.35 p.m. trackless which left Stephenson Place at that time, travelled to Brampton, returning from this terminus at 7.50 p.m., and proceeded to New Whittington from town at 8 00 p.m. This unidentified trolley vehicle left New Whittington at 8.25 p.m. and its journey terminated at the Thornfield Depot at 8.45 p.m. Hoggard pointed out in his letter that the conductor mis-punched the Chesterfield/Brampton and Brampton/Chesterfield tickets down the wrong sides. A copy of this letter is included in the illustrations.

The two single-deckers 8 and 20 were suitably bedizened for their final apearance, with striped bunting on the fronts, roofs, bodies and lifeguards, and flags adorning the trolleypoles. Each bore a frontal shield studded with light bulbs, bearing the coat-of-arms in a smaller shield, and carrying the words 'CHESTERFIELD CORPORATION TRANSPORT 1927-1938' while each destination indicator displayed the illuminated letters 'R.I.P.'

'With ceremonial befitting the departure of old friends' gushed the *Times*, displaying a warmth not noticeable in the past 'Chesterfield bade farewell to its trolleybuses last night, when two of the buses carried a party of members and officials of the Corporation on the last journey over the route from Brampton to New Whittington.' Around fifty of the privileged took their seats at Stephenson Place, including the Mayor, Alderman Harry Hatton, and the triumvirate of Robinson, Cropper and Hoggard. A large crowd, anxious to speed the veteran and its junior partner on their way, saw the loaded REVs glide away towards Brampton, brilliantly lit in the darkness of the March evening. It was appropriate that Bill Hardwick was one of the two drivers selected for the honour of manning the buses, the other driver being Jack Owen. For the last time they swung around the Brampton loop and headed back down Chatsworth Road, following the trail of the old tramcars many years before. The town centre welcomed them for their final journey before they moved silently along Sheffield Road, round the Whittington circle and on to New Whittington via the hill once thought beyond their capabilities by their detractors in council. The Stone Lane reverser was engaged for one last turn, before the two decorated conveyances, in close line-astern, switched trolleys to the opposite line at Hardwick Street and ran smoothly into the depot from the rear as they had done countless times before. Their ultimate trip had logged 10.7 miles exactly. All along the route throngs of townspeople gave them a fond farewell as they rolled past for the final time to culminate the trackless period in Chesterfield's transport history.

On returning to the garage the party were treated to refreshments in the employees recreation room. There is no record of any souvenir tickets being dispensed on the journey though the presence of conductors on both buses suggests that they might have been. Alderman Robinson gave a short speech extolling the virtues of the replacement fleet, assuring the company that in five years all Corporation vehicles would run on diesel oil. Finally the mayor presented Robinson with a silver cigarette box engraved with a representation of Straker 12, as a souvenir of the occasion. The inscription ran:

PRESENTED TO
ALDERMAN PHILIP ROBINSON JP
CHAIRMAN OF THE
CHESTERFIELD CORPORATION TRANSPORT COMMITTEE
IN COMMEMORATION OF THE OCCASION OF THE
LAST TROLLEY BUS RUN IN CHESTERFIELD
THURSDAY 24TH MARCH 1938

The final trackless year, terminating just one week short of the full twelve months, saw the buses complete 631,827 miles, transporting 5,860,647 people. Costs included £194 on the overhead, £1,862 on the chassis and bodies, and £635 on tyre replacement. Traffic revenue was £34,595, with £35 for parcels and £67 on advertising. The fourteen Strakers all totalled mileages in the 34,000 to 39,000 bracket, 12 topping the list with 39,069, while 2 was bottom with 34,243. The two Ransomes weighed in with 30,600 miles each, and the Karriers remained definitely underused, with 18 running 15,500 miles, 19 19,382 and 20 24,733.

There was definitely no ceremony or sentimentality associated with the disposal of the trackless fleet; space was needed in the garage for the sixteen replacement gearless Titan TD5C double-deckers, and all the nineteen REVs had been pushed out into the field adjoining the depot by the next morning. Some had undoubtedly been dumped earlier in the week, as a photograph in Friday's *Times* showed forlorn rows of the discarded vehicles already lined up. Figures published in the newspaper showed the debt owed by the department to the trolleybuses. During their eleven-year service they had covered 6,128,675 miles, transporting 60,665,903 travellers and producing receipts amounting to £354,502. They had paid off the outstanding debt on the old trams, plus the road reinstatement after the lifting of the rails, plus their own purchase costs.

A few comments in the local press related to the demise of electric traction. Perhaps those most pleased with their departure were wireless enthusiasts along the route, who could now sit back and listen to their favourite programmes uninterrupted by the interference which announced each trolley vehicle passing by. Those living on Sheffield Road in particular could determine the exact time the first REV left the depot, and peace on the airwaves was only restored when the service ceased for the night. It was also felt that passengers would not miss the sudden stops and starts, risking dislocation of necks!

The removal of the Strakers must have taken some time, as a photograph taken later in the year, with full leaf on the surrounding trees, still showed them parked in the field where they had been unceremoniously shoved, with their identifying motifs now painted out. At the 17 May committee meeting Hoggard was empowered to sell off the remaining trolleybuses, plus the 26.7 tons of lead-covered cable removed from the ducts between the electricity works and town. However, at the June gathering the sale was deferred 'for the time being.' The cable was sold in September for £500, and by this time the Strakers had presumably been removed. On 22 November Hoggard submitted tenders for the surviving trackless, and the five relatively modern buses, with many years' service still left in them, were sold off to the Steel Breaking & Dismantling Co. of Lockoford Lane, Chesterfield, for the ludicrous sum of £80 10s! This should be contrasted with the £707 paid for the three Karriers in late 1935. Perhaps the committee were embarrassed by their unwanted presence at Thornfield, but there is no doubt they were vended for a pittance, and their disposal did no credit for those responsible for their summary fate.

The total lack of interest in the preservation of the railless made it certain that only photographs serve as their memorials, though both the horse and electric cars fared better, with the survival of Horse Car 8, refurbished in Chesterfield, and the rebuilding and restoration of Electric Car 7 at Crich. Both conveyances can be seen at the National Tramway Museum, venerable transport artefacts still existing not far from the Derbyshire town where they originally performed their useful functions for the benefit of the public. Long may they continue to do so.

A fine study of Karrier 20 leading out Straker 8 at Thornfield on the last day of trolleybus operation. Both buses are suitably bedecked in valedictory trappings, with bunting and illuminated frontal shields. Note the 'R.I.P' in the destination windows, and Richard Hoggard, in obligatory bowler hat, in the entrance door of the Straker. (*F.J. Seaman*)

Closure time again, and the usual suspects line up in front of a well-lit Straker 8 after the terminal run on the evening of 24 March. The ubiquitous Bill Hardwick is the driver, while front row, left to right, can be seen Alderman Cropper, Mayor Harry Hatton, and Philip Robinson. Alderman Varley and Hoggard occupy the step behind. *(F.J. Seaman)*

Councillors and others pose on the opposite side of No.8, all keen to get in shot, though the car crew on the right appear to be from Karrier 20, including the tall figure of Driver Owen. *(F.J. Seaman)*

90

*Right:* Silver cigarette case with an engraving of Straker 12, presented to Philip Robinson at the above gathering to commemorate the demise of railless traction in Chesterfield.

**Chesterfield Corporation Transport Department**

ENCLOSURE

R. HOGGARD, M.INST.T.
GENERAL MANAGER

Telephone Nos. 2357, 2051.
and 2301 Ext. 53.

Your reference .........................
Our reference. RH/ ASC
In any reply, please quote
our reference.

Thornfield Depot.,
Sheffield Road,
Chesterfield.

_____29th March,____193 8.

Alderman P. M. Robinson, J.P.,
Portland Works,
CHESTERFIELD.

Dear Mr. Chairman,

Last run on Chesterfield Trolley 'Bus
-------------------------------------------

I have pleasure in forwarding herewith the last tickets issued on the last Trolley 'Bus Run in Chesterfield on March 24th, 1938.

Tickets 61B 0433, 50V 0312, 84Y 5688 were the last tickets issued from Chesterfield to Brampton 7.35 p.m. journey.

Tickets 61B 0434, 50V 0313, 84Y 5690 were the last tickets issued Brampton to Chesterfield 7.50 p.m. journey.

Unfortunately the Conductor issuing these tickets punched them on the wrong side.

You will notice the 3 tickets Chesterfield to Brampton are punched on the inward side, Brampton to Chesterfield on the outward side. This, I am sorry, was not pointed out until it was too late.

Ticket 61B 0435, 50V 0314, 84Y 5691, 84F 9066, 96D 2291, 94A 9409 are the last tickets issued Chesterfield to New Whittington on the 8 p.m. journey.

Ticket 61B 0436, 50V 0315, 84Y 5692 and 84F 9067 are the last tickets issued New Whittington to the Garage at 8.25 p.m., the last trolley 'bus running into the Garage at 8.45 p.m.

P.T.O.

*Left:* A letter sent by Hoggard to Robinson on 29 March lists the tickets vended on the last service run of the trackless on the 24th. The tickets are now preserved in the Local Studies Library. (*Local Studies Library*)

*Below:* A poignant line-up of the redundant fleet which appeared in the *Derbyshire Times* on 25 March, only one day after abandonment, showing the two Ransomes, 16 and 17, with Strakers 10 and 11 on the right, and 3 behind. Straker 6 appears on the extreme left. Note Thornfield House looming behind the leafless trees. (*Chesterfield Borough*)

Some of the brand-new Titan TD5C gearless diesel buses posed for the camera at Thornfield as replacements for the discarded REVs. The nearest bears a Leyland advert in the upstairs window. *(F.J. Seaman)*

The unwanted vehicles, still awaiting collection by Devey Bros, linger on into the spring of 1938. In the left foreground is one of the last cars, No.8, with 4 alongside. Straker 12 can be glimpsed in the next rank. *(A.R. Kaye)*

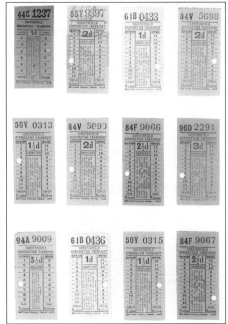

Penny white 44C 1237 was one of the first tickets issued on the trackless, being handed out on the opening journey of Straker 1 on 23 May 1927. Green 2d 86Y 9397 was issued on Straker 4 on supposedly the last service run on 24 March 1938. It is signed by the driver, Gilsthorpe, and conductor, Clarke. However a further REV followed 4, and the rest of the tickets were distributed on this vehicle. See the letter on page 91 for details. Colours are 1d white, 1½d pink, 2d green, 2½d brown, 3d red, 3½d orange.

# TICKETS AND FARES

In September 1927, after trolleybus replacement of the trams, the undertaking changed its name to the Chesterfield Transport Department, and tickets were amended to carry that name. Issues given out on the last tram/first railless journey included 1d examples with six stages, and a block date of 6.25, and 2d ones dated 3.27 with ten stages. A fares schedule from 1928 shows the following prices for trolleybus travel:

1d        Brampton-Heaton Street/Barker Lane
1½d      Brampton-Foljambe Road
2d        Brampton-Stephenson Place

1d        Whittington-Nelson Street / Hare and Hounds
1½d      Whittington-Albert Street
2d        Whittington-Market Place

Workmens' fares were ½d less than the above over all stages.

When the trolleybus extension to New Whittington was operational in 1929, fares were set as follows:

| | Whittington Moor | Cock & Magpie | Brierley Street | New Whittington |
|---|---|---|---|---|
| Chesterfield | 2d | 3d | 3½d | 4d |
| Hare & Hounds | 1d | 2d | 3d | 3d |
| Nelson Street | 1d | 2d | 2½d | 3d |
| Whittington Moor | | 1d | 1½d | 2d |
| Cock & Magpie | | | 1d | 1½d |
| Brierley Street | | | | 1d |

Again Workmens' fares were ½d below the ordinary fare.

In November 1929 the ordinary fare between the Hare and Hounds and Brierley Street was reduced to 2½d. Workmens' fares between town and Brierley Street and town to the New Whittington terminus were also cut by ½d in each case. From 1 April 1935 fares on the Whittington section were again lowered by ½d over each stage. The through journey from town to New Whittington was set at 3½d. These prices remained in force until trolleybus operation ceased. The tickets issued on the last service run on 24 March show the styles then in use. All tickets of 1d, 1½d, 2d, 2½d and 3d denominations have twelve stages, with Child and Workman sections at the bottom. The 3½d example by contrast lists only nine stages. It is uncertain whether any tickets were given out on the last official ride on the evening of 24 March 1938; no examples have yet come to light.

# WIRING DIAGRAMS

Four of these survive in the Borough archives. A shows the turning loop at West Bars by the Market Place Railway Station. B shows the Whittington Moor turning loop after the 1929 modification for REVs running through to New Whittington. C shows the one-way system operating in the town centre. D shows the reverser at Stone Lane, New Whittington.

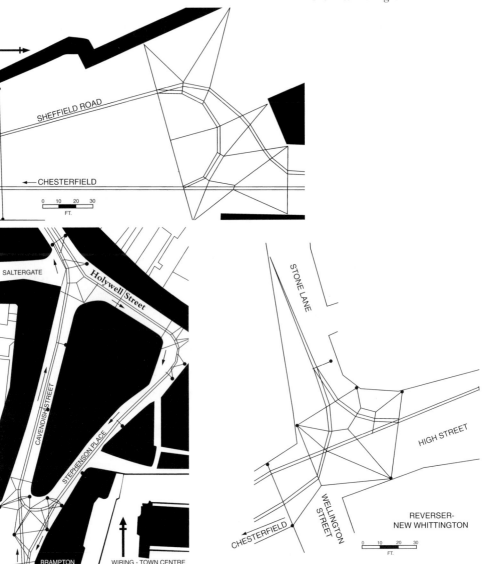

TOWN CENTRE

←BRAMPTON

FT.

0  20  40  60
FT.
WIRING - WEST BARS

SHEFFIELD ROAD

←CHESTERFIELD

0  10  20  30
FT.

SALTERGATE

Holywell Street

CAVENDISH STREET

STEPHENSON PLACE

BRAMPTON          WIRING - TOWN CENTRE

STONE LANE

HIGH STREET

CHESTERFIELD

WELLINGTON STREET

REVERSER-
NEW WHITTINGTON

0  10  20  30
FT.

# APPENDICES

## TROLLEYBUSES (23 May 1927-24 March 1938)

| FLEET NO. | YEAR | CHASSIS | BODY | TYPE/SEATING |
|---|---|---|---|---|
| 1-14* | 1927 | Straker-Clough | Reeve & Kenning | B32C |
| 16-17 | 1931 | Ransomes D2 | Ransomes | L48R |
| 18-20+ | 1935 | Karrier-Clough | Roe | B32R |

*No.13 was renumbered 15 on 17 June 1928
+Originally York 30 – 32. Built 1931

## TROLLEYBUS REGISTRATIONS

| FLEET NO. | REG. NO. | HACKNEY CARRIAGE NO. | FIRST RAN | LAST RAN |
|---|---|---|---|---|
| 1 | RA 1810 | 231 | 23. 5. 27 | 23. 3. 38 |
| 2 | RA 1811 | 262 | 23.5.27 | 24.3.38 |
| 3 | RA 1812 | 253 | 23.5.27 | 23.3.38 |
| 4 | RA 1813 | 254 | 28.5.27 | 24.3.38 |
| 5 | RA 1814 | 255 | 23.5.27 | 24.3.38 |
| 6 | RA 1815 | 256 | 23.5.27 | 1.3.38 |
| 7 | RA 1816 | 257 | 23.5.27 | 24.3.38 |
| 8 | RA 1817 | 161 | 30.7.27 | LAST CAR |
| 9 | RA 1819 | 371 | 29.7.27 | 23.3.38 |
| 10 | RA 1820 | 391 | 29.7.27 | 23.3.38 |
| 11 | RA 1821 | 263 | 28.7.27 | 23.3.38 |
| 12 | RA 1822 | 264 | 27.7.27 | 24.3.38 |
| 13/15 | RA 1823 | 265 | 13.8.27 | 24.3.38 |
| 14 | RA 1824 | 266 | 13.8.27 | 24.3.38 |
| 16 | RB 4890 | 391 | 2.12.31 | 19.3.38 |
| 17 | RB 4891 | 394 | 5.12.31 | 19.3.38 |
| 18 | VY 2291 | ? | 6.12.35 | 23.3.38 |
| 19 | VY 2292 | ? | 7.12.35 | 18.3.38 |
| 20 | VY 2293 | ? | 7.12.35 | LAST CAR |

## TROLLEYBUS MILEAGES

| REV. NO. | 1927-8 | 1928-9 | 1929-30 | 1930-1 | 1931-2 | 1932-3 | 1933-4 | 1934-5 |
|---|---|---|---|---|---|---|---|---|
| 1 | 26,429 | 33,149 | 37,650 | 41,947 | 41,524 | 37,548 | 38,961 | 39,032 |
| 2 | 24,774 | 32,581 | 36,975 | 39,860 | 43,114 | 39,444 | 36,892 | 39,885 |
| 3 | 27,852 | 32,043 | 38,101 | 41,518 | 41,141 | 40,050 | 34,672 | 37,555 |
| 4 | 24,811 | 32,897 | 37,463 | 42,360 | 39,938 | 38,464 | 34,577 | 37,914 |
| 5 | 28,604 | 31,642 | 36,640 | 42,541 | 41,886 | 39,004 | 36,217 | 38,912 |
| 6 | 27,089 | 31,566 | 39,075 | 41,310 | 43,370 | 39,297 | 36,078 | 37,201 |
| 7 | 28,386 | 33,983 | 38,411 | 42,768 | 43,681 | 38,920 | 38,651 | 37,468 |
| 8 | 21,258 | 33,989 | 36,965 | 41,705 | 43,026 | 37,558 | 36,979 | 38,597 |
| 9 | 22,429 | 31,234 | 33,850 | 20,196 | 18,430 | 13,631 | 26,538 | 32,790 |
| 10 | 22,945 | 33,032 | 37,835 | 40,958 | 42,412 | 40,904 | 35,668 | 36,458 |
| 11 | 21,807 | 34,696 | 37,242 | 30,357 | 23,002 | 18,468 | 25,325 | 33,658 |
| 12 | 20,894 | 33,801 | 33,781 | 44,928 | 40,652 | 38,727 | 38,689 | 37,812 |
| 13/15 | 21,310 | 33,747 | 37,827 | 42,853 | 41,833 | 38,797 | 35,820 | 35,951 |
| 14 | 20,092 | 33,301 | 39,130 | 44,047 | 42,651 | 39,339 | 38,402 | 39,058 |
| 16 | | | | 12,049 | 39,333 | 43,080 | 43,080 | 44,233 |
| 17 | | | | 10,756 | 40,529 | 41,220 | 41,220 | 40,198 |
| TOTALS | 338,681 | 461,842 | 520,946 | 557,348 | 574,926 | 580,015 | 588,536 | 606,806 |

| | 1935-6 | 1936-7 | 1937-8 | TOTAL |
|---|---|---|---|---|
| 1 | 36,616 | 34,551 | 36,301 | 403,709 |
| 2 | 34,595 | 32,364 | 34,243 | 394,727 |
| 3 | 37,911 | 33,985 | 36,256 | 402,884 |
| 4 | 35,952 | 34,664 | 36,086 | 395,126 |
| 5 | 36,575 | 34,411 | 35,423 | 401,854 |
| 6 | 39,082 | 36,191 | 36,503 | 406,842 |
| 7 | 36,925 | 33,825 | 36,438 | 409,522 |
| 8 | 36,579 | 33,302 | 37,407 | 397,361 |
| 9 | 37,212 | 31,311 | 34,783 | 302,405 |
| 10 | 37,894 | 34,646 | 38,370 | 401,123 |
| 11 | 36,485 | 35,576 | 35,083 | 331,699 |

| | 1935-6 | 1936-7 | 1937-8 | TOTAL |
|---|---|---|---|---|
| 12 | 37,622 | 33,498 | 39,069 | 399,473 |
| 14 | 37,895 | 33,943 | 37,122 | 404,982 |
| 15 | 35,890 | 35,090 | 37,786 | 396,905 |
| 16 | 42,074 | 44,649 | 30,680 | 256,098 |
| 17 | 43,406 | 44,016 | 30,663 | 250,788 |
| 18 | 8,586 | 22,751 | 15,500 | 46,837 |
| 19 | 8,449 | 25,285 | 19,382 | 53,116 |
| 20 | 8,361 | 24,304 | 24,733 | 57,399 |
| TOTALS | 629,387 | 638,363 | 631,827 | TOTAL MILEAGE 1927-1938 = 6,128,675 |

## DEMONSTRATOR MILEAGES (Included in the above figures)

| | REG. NO. | YEAR | MILEAGE | FIRST RAN | LAST RAN |
|---|---|---|---|---|---|
| ENGLISH ELECTRIC | CK 3898 | 1928 | 179 | 16.6.28 | 19.6.28 |
| LEYLAND TBD1 | OV 1175 | 1931 | 5,461 | 22.8.31 | 18.10.31 |
| LEYLAND TBS1 | TJ 2822 | 1933 | 8,964 | 19.9.33 | 11.12.33 |
| LEYLAND TB10 | ATD 747 | 1935-6 | 1,278 | 29.11.35 | 1.1.36 |

TOTAL MILEAGE = 1,582

## TROLLEYBUS STATISTICS

| YEAR | PASSENGERS | EXPENDITURE (£) | | | RECEIPTS (£) | | |
|---|---|---|---|---|---|---|---|
| | | OH | REVS | TYRES | TRAFFIC | ADVERTS | PARCELS |
| 1928 | 4,060,445 | 63 | 1,319 | 1,354 | 23,519 | 10 | 42 |
| 1929 | 4,968,062 | 593 | 1,379 | 1,495 | 28,267 | 51 | 36 |
| 1930 | 5,702,884 | 769 | 2,352 | 1,628 | 33,384 | 221 | 46 |
| 1931 | 5,677,842 | 586 | 2,539 | 975 | 33,231 | 182 | 42 |
| 1932 | 5,744,730 | 621 | 2,099 | 790 | 33,768 | 182 | 33 |
| 1933 | 5,533,188 | 633 | 2,123 | 670 | 32,397 | 182 | 26 |
| 1934 | 5,552,016 | 242 | 2,040 | 438 | 32,661 | 149 | 26 |
| 1935 | 5,640,405 | 342 | 2,486 | 568 | 33,075 | 53 | 32 |
| 1936 | 5,879,421 | 359 | 2,024 | 593 | 34,005 | 48 | 37 |
| 1937 | 6,006,998 | 169 | 1,997 | 590 | 35,131 | 72 | 39 |
| 1938 | 5,860,647 | 194 | 1,862 | 635 | 34,595 | 67 | 35 |

TOTAL PASSENGERS CARRIED = 60,665,903

# BIBLIOGRAPHY

BOOKS
B.M. Marsden, *Chesterfield Trams and Trolleybuses* (KM, 1984)
           *Tramtracks and Trolleybooms* (Amadeus, 1988)
           *A Chesterfield Tramscape* (Ryestone Press, 2001)
W.G. Marks, *Chesterfield Tramways 1879-1927* (Chesterfield Borough Council, 1927)
Transpire, *Tramlines to Fleetlines* (Chesterfield Borough Council, 1982)
T.F. Wright, *History of Chesterfield Vol. IV* (Chesterfield Borough Council, 1992)

ARTICLES
*Chesterfield's New Transport System*, W.G. Marks (Tramway and Railway World, 13 October 1927)
*The Organisation of a Town's Bus Service*, W.G. Marks (The Commercial Motor, 30 October 1928)
*Reconstruction of York Trolleybus Route*, (Tramway and Railway World, 14 January 1931)
*Double-Deck Trolleybuses for Chesterfield* (As above)

OTHER SOURCES
Chesterfield Borough Archives 1912-1938
Chesterfield Tramways/Transport Commitee Minutes 1912-1938
Derbyshire Times 1912-1938
Former Chesterfield Transport Department Records
Local Studies Department, Chesterfield Library